Heart Song

ISBN: 978-0-9568237-2-4

Stephen Shaw's Books

Visit the website: www.i-am-stephen-shaw.com

I Am contains spiritual and mystical teachings from enlightened masters that point the way to love, peace, bliss, freedom and spiritual awakening.

Heart Song takes you on a mystical adventure into creating your reality and manifesting your dreams, and reveals the secrets to attaining a fulfilled and joyful life.

They Walk Among Us is a love story spanning two realities. Explore the mystery of the angels. Discover the secrets of Love Whispering.

The Other Side explores the most fundamental question in each reality. What happens when the physical body dies? Where do you go? Expand your awareness. Journey deep into the Mystery.

Reflections offers mystical words for guidance, meditation and contemplation. Open the book anywhere and unwrap your daily inspiration.

5D is the Fifth Dimension. Discover ethereal doorways hidden in the fabric of space-time. Seek the advanced mystical teachings.

Star Child offers an exciting glimpse into the future on earth. The return of the gods and the advanced mystical teachings. And the ultimate battle of light versus darkness.

The Tribe expounds the joyful creation of new Earth. What happened after the legendary battle of Machu Picchu? What is Christ consciousness? What is Ecstatic Tantra?

The Fractal Key reveals the secrets of the shamans. This handbook for psychonauts discloses the techniques and practices used in psychedelic healing and transcendent journeys.

I never feel like I fit in anywhere. I never feel like I truly belong.

"Are you coming down for dinner, honey?"

My only moments of peace occur during this precious time alone, brushing my hair in front of the mirror. The way mother used to brush my hair.

"Zara?"

"Yes, dear, on my way."

It's my thirty-fourth birthday next week and here I am, feeling so unhappy.

I walk downstairs and give him a kiss. Robert has prepared a magnificent candle-lit dinner; he smiles and pours me a glass of Cabernet Sauvignon. I gaze at him across the table. He is a good man, kind, caring, loving, committed. It should be enough. My life should be enough.

"Are you alright, sweetheart?"

"Yes. I was just thinking about mother."

He looks at me gently: "Grieving is a natural process. Grief takes its own time to dissipate."

I nod. Of course, he is right.

I gaze thoughtfully at my dinner. Losing mother a few months ago was painful; she filled my world with such love, affection and direction. If it wasn't for her, I would never have met Robert, would never have studied accountancy. She helped me so much; guided me so strongly. I feel so grateful and … guilty.

Why on earth do I feel guilty? Oh my, is there anger too? I am supposed to feel sad, nothing but sad. I should be crying all the time! Why did she leave me? What am I supposed to do on my own?

I never used to think about death. In my twenties I was invincible – full of life, energy and vitality. It felt like there were so many possibilities and such a great future ahead of me. I remember watching Bon Jovi singing: "It's my life, it's now or never, I ain't gonna live forever, I just want to live while I'm alive!"

By now I was supposed to have the perfect love, marriage, a family, the white picket fence and a couple of dogs.

Dinner is a rather sedate affair. Later I am lying in bed next to Robert. He drops off to sleep within minutes, as always, while I am staring at the ceiling again. Why can't I disappear into dreamland too?

* * *

In the morning it's off to work. Another day of drudgery: crunching numbers to please a boss who always seems moody; saying the right thing to a difficult secretary so she doesn't put my paperwork at the bottom of her pile; attending meeting after meeting; trying to be friendly to colleagues and cordial to clients. Wondering when this whirlwind will ever slow down.

My phone beeps. It's Robert reminding me that he is away on business for the next few days. *I am on my own!* I text him back, writing that I will miss him, asking him to take care and come home safely.

I glance at the clock. There is just enough time to rush out and get bubble bath, candles and my favourite salmon salad. Tonight the world will stop turning. It's a bliss I am deeply anticipating.

Two hours later it is just me, with my music, and tea-light candles scattered everywhere, eating salmon salad, drinking wine, reading a gossipy entertainment magazine, luxuriating in the steamy water. No one to please, no one to appease, no compromises.

For once I feel calm and relaxed. Why do I feel such peace when Robert is gone? I need his love and affection and enjoy our conversations ... and I like being in a relationship.

The soft sound makes me turn my head. A gentle and beautiful melody is emanating from the direction of the bedroom. I turn off my music and listen. Is it coming from outside? Where is the source of that exquisite sound? I'm all wrinkly now, so I clamber out the bath and wrap a huge, fleecy towel around me.

There is a silver-blue light glimmering in the bedroom. The wood-framed mirror appears to be exuding a gentle glow over my wingback chair. I can still hear that sweet sound but cannot locate it. Sitting down, I throw the towel to one side and gaze at my damp body: long auburn hair; sparkling green eyes; full breasts; smooth tummy; and natural curves which I like very much. A warm feeling dances along my thighs, producing that familiar sensual tingle.

Mother used to spend ages brushing my long hair, and I felt so loved and adored in those moments. I lean forward to inspect my fringe ... there is a slight giddiness ... is it the wine?

The mirror seems alive with subtle, shimmering wavelets … my image is melting away … in its place a silver, sensual woman flows before me.

Hello, I am Tethys. I hear the soft, feminine voice. It does not startle me. I feel wonderfully tipsy and strangely serene.

I am the one who flows through your forests, beneath your earth and along your mountain ridges. I am the stream, the lake, the waterfall, the rain, the river and the ocean. I am the water-goddess.

I am giggling as I reply: "Hello, Te-th-ys! Do you mind if I call you Ripple? Te-th-ys does not roll easily off my tongue. Not tonight anyway."

I recognise your loneliness. I understand your pain and frustration. Do you know that you are a goddess waiting to be reborn?

And with that drop of wisdom swirling in my consciousness, I finally surrender to gorgeous fatigue. My huge bed welcomes me and I quickly drift away under the soft feathers … and into a world of nebulous dreams.

* * *

Why didn't I close those shutters? So bright … My eyes open slowly to the morning rays. What a deep sleep, and not even a headache.

I reach for my fluffy pink dressing gown. Coffee is calling me. Day? Ah, Friday. What a relief. I stumble down to the kitchen; it's quiet, I am alone, how lovely.

It's getting autumnal so I opt for warming porridge; and then the daily decision: Which outfit will make me feel good?

Soon I am dressed and ready; no time to sit and stare, except for the few minutes it takes to arrange my hair. I pick up my brush … and the mirror begins swirling … a flashback to last night. No, it can't be! Staring back at me is a gorgeous silver woman.

I drop my brush. I feel sick and dizzy. Am I ill? What is happening?

Hello, Zara, nice to see you again. Do not be afraid.

Oh my, it's too much work, the constant stress. Now I am hallucinating.

Trust your intuition. Reach out slowly and touch me. You will sense that I am very real.

My mind is confused; part of me is panicking, the other part is unnaturally calm. Blindly I reach out and allow my fingertips to graze the flowing form. It's wet! How can it be wet? My mother's death has finally tipped me over the edge.

I reach in deeper. Everything in my mirror is flowing, undulating liquid. Impossible! Yet there she is: a floating, silver, semi-translucent woman looking back at me.

"Am I going mad?"

There are many portals into other worlds. Only gods and goddesses can open and close these portals. This is part of the greater reality.

I had better phone in sick. Something is not right. Either I have lost it or something incredible is taking place. There is no way I will be able to work today.

"What is happening? What do you want?"

I am offering you the opportunity to create a beautiful reality. A journey to a fulfilled and joyful life.

"No, no, no! *This* is real life. I go to work five days a week. I work long hours in a profession I enjoy. I am financially secure. I love Robert!"

I hear her gentle, swirling voice. *Life is whatever you choose. There are many realities beyond your own. There are so many possibilities.*

"Go away! This is not real. It can't be happening!"

I throw my hairbrush at the mirror; there is a faint splashing sound and she is gone. I reach out to touch the hard glass and my reflection blazes back at me.

If you want a taste of happiness, if you wish to discover how joyful and loving your life can be, meet me at the lake near your aunt's house. I will be waiting.

I put my hands over my ears and hum a tune. This has to end soon.

* * *

I grew up in London. I am a sensible, modern woman, adept at handling challenging situations. What is going on with me? Perhaps I am still reeling with grief and anxiety. I don't know what to think. I need to talk to someone.

I phone my quirky aunt and she picks up after three rings. We exchange pleasantries for a while and finally I tell her how stressed I am. "When can I come and visit, Lilura?" There is a brief pause, then, "Anytime, honey. I am free all weekend. Would you like to travel up today?"

I don't need a second invitation. "Yes, please, that would be wonderful. Shall I arrive about five o'clock this evening?"

"Sounds perfect. I will prepare something nice for dinner. See you later, sweetie."

My aunt lives in the gorgeous Lake District, commonly known as The Lakes, in North West England. It contains the deepest and longest lakes in England as well as plenty of charming mountains (also known as 'fells'). The majority of the area was designated as the Lake District National Park in 1951. It is the largest of the thirteen National Parks in England and Wales, and the second largest in the UK.

It's about six hours' drive, so I scramble to tidy the house, collect my things and pack an overnight bag. An hour later I am in the car singing loudly to my favourite tunes and moving like a sprite dancing on a rainbow.

The tyres finally crunch onto her gravel driveway; a warm feeling envelops me as sweet memories from childhood flood back. The quaint three-bedroom cottage has not changed much. The front garden is strewn with brightly coloured flowers in various stages of bloom and surrounded by miles of green fields, tall trees and rolling hills. It is an idyllic setting to regain my composure.

Lilura's voice rings out from the kitchen door. "Hey, honey! Come inside, come inside." I walk in, drop my bag on the floor and share a close embrace. "Lovely to see you, dear. It's been a long time."

"Way too long. Sorry. Life in London seems so hectic and one gets carried away by it all."

"You must be exhausted from the drive. Cup of tea? I have some nice home-made biscuits. Sit down, sit down, there's so much to catch up. Tell me everything that's been happening with you."

She is flustering around the kitchen, switching on the kettle, arranging the side plates, opening a tin of biscuits and deciding on the tea options. "Redbush or peppermint or –"

"Redbush is fine. Black, one sugar, please."

She proffers a plate of stem ginger cookies bathed in dark chocolate. I nod, then begin to warm up the conversation by talking about my relationship with Robert. I hear my voice droning on about my wonderful home life, but it feels like I am a spectator to the words. She listens patiently, muttering a gentle "hmm" here and there.

"More tea, dear?"

I shake my head and look at the floor tiles. She touches my hand and looks kindly at me. "What's really going on, Zara?" Suddenly my veneer trembles and my eyes cloud; I am mumbling with emotions spilling all over the place.

"Mother's death has thrown me into turmoil. I cried huge spasms for the first few weeks, now I am left questioning everything. She guided me, showed me the way forward at every stage; now I feel lost and confused. I don't know what I am doing ..."

Lilura is gazing at me with a wonderful compassionate expression. She seems to understand. I relax and take a chance.

"Now I am seeing things, hallucinations, a being in a mirror, impossible I know. I am sure it's just stress, overwork or grief. Robert says I need time, time to grieve, time to adapt."

And then I am gushing about the woman in the mirror, my frustration about my relationship, my inability to sleep for more than a few hours, the sheer boredom at work, my entire life that seems all wrong. Where's it all coming from? I don't even share this much with Robert.

After an hour of intermittent tears and a waterfall of words and emotions, I start feeling very tired. Perhaps it is the long drive, perhaps it is the country air.

Lilura lights the fire in her cosy front room. A bottle of red wine has been warming by the hearth; she passes it over: Vive l'Evolution Cotes du Roussillon Villages. "Yes, please," I say. She leaves the corkscrew and glasses with me and disappears into the kitchen.

A few minutes later she returns with two trays of delicious delight: "Boeuf bourguignon – perfect autumn comfort food." Through the window I see the sun setting amidst a haze of clouds. It is truly beautiful here.

She has been so kind and patient with me. Although she has not said much, I feel listened to and understood. I am floating somewhere between deeply relaxed and mildly exhausted. It's no surprise that within the hour I am tucked up in the guest bedroom with my book. I manage no more than half a page before sleep deftly overtakes me.

* * *

It is morning and I waken to the chirrup of birds, an unfamiliar sound to a city woman. I glance at the sheep grazing in the distance. The window is open a crack and a light breeze dances around me. A cup of steaming coffee is already on the bedside table. Sweet aunt!

The entire weekend lies before me. What a blissful thought. I lay in bed for a while, catching up on my reading, then spring into a billowing shower. At the breakfast table Lilura suggests we go for a walk to the lake, which is about a mile away. The sun is shining and the sky is clear. I agree immediately.

It's an enjoyable amble across green fields, dodging a herd of cows, meandering through a bit of forest ... and now we are here ... standing before the stunning expanse of light blue water. The cool air drifting across the lake is invigorating and I fill my lungs with long, deep breaths. It's so peaceful.

There is a wooden bench close to the lake edge. We sit for a while and gaze at the still water. A covey of ducks waddles past. The sun is warm on our shoulders. "Your grandfather built this bench. Lasted all these years."

My mother's parents grew up here and Lilura never left the family home. Mother moved to London, the exciting city of bright lights and opportunity. I sigh softly. As for my father ... the mystery man I never knew ... the man no one would ever talk about. I often wonder if he broke mother's heart. Perhaps that is why I am an only child.

"Lilura, what do you know about –"

A sudden commotion on the water distracts us. No more than a few yards away a small eddy is forming, and slowly the whirling water rises from the lake. A curvaceous figure is appearing. No, it can't be! This can't be happening here.

I look at my aunt; she is not moving and her face reveals only calmness. I grab her hand. "Don't be afraid, dear," she says in a soothing voice.

Hello, Zara, I am Tethys, the daughter of Gaia, primordial earth-goddess. Thank you for making the journey to see me.

My teeth are clenched. Why is Lilura not saying anything? Does she know this being?

I wish to connect with you and share my wisdom. No harm will come to you.

I am staring at this water-goddess. Lilura is firmly holding my hand. Long moments pass. I try to calm my breathing.

Let me know when you are ready.

My aunt looks at me gently. "It's time, Zara. Your mother left so you could truly find yourself, so you could step into your life. Trust the water-goddess. Everything will be alright."

I look at the strange and radiant being. This is beyond my current understanding but Lilura has always acted in my best interests. My intuition begins to override my fearful mind. It's time to let go and surrender into something new. I let out a deep sigh. "I am ready."

To begin your journey, you will need a **notebook** *or* **journal**. *You cannot go any further without this. You may personalise it and make it something special. Place a photo on the cover, write your name on it, give it a title, anything you like.*

Lilura winks at me. Smiling, she pulls a beautiful, large journal from her bag. It is covered in maroon cloth and embroidered on the front in dark blue letters: Zara's Journal. I look at her in surprise ... my hands gently caress the soft material ... such a thoughtful gift ... it falls open and I trace my fingers along the white lined pages. There is a stylish blue pen reposing in the spine.

"It's time to discover *you*," my aunt says softly. "I am off for a walk; see you later at the cottage."

So here I am, sitting on a wooden bench at the lake edge, about to start a lesson with a water-goddess. It all seems so natural to Lilura. As for me, I smile quietly at the curious and unfamiliar reality that I am about to embrace.

* * *

Tethys shimmers and flows on the lake just in front of me. She presumably belongs to the water and cannot move any closer.

The sun is soaking into my skin and the soothing sound of ripples lulls me into quietude.

Let's begin. Open your journal to the first page.

"It's quite surreal conversing with a water-being."

You will get used to it. People have an extraordinary ability to adapt to new realities. Now let's talk about your cage.

"My cage?"

Use this heading: **My Cage**. *You can make notes as we talk. Let's think about your current reality. How did you arrive here? What were your influences? Who guided you?*

"My mother was my greatest influence. I knew my father only briefly; he left when I was about three. Mother pushed me toward a profession which she felt would be economically secure. I work as an accountant in a small firm. She was very helpful in getting me through my studies which, to be honest, I found rather challenging.

"I grew up in London, a thriving and busy city, so I quickly learned to handle an exciting and demanding environment. The city tends to instil drive, ambition and a sense of competition."

Do you love what you do?

"I am good at my job. I put in long hours. I earn enough to be comfortable. But ... no ... I don't love it ... it's just a job."

How do you expect to find fulfilment and happiness when you spend a huge slice of your time doing something you don't love?

"I don't know. I am just trying to fit into this world in the best way I understand. I have to earn a living and pay the accounts. What else is there?"

Tethys is quiet for a while, giving me time to reflect. Mother did the best she could, encouraged me into a safe profession. There was only the two of us. I learned early that you need money to survive in this tough world. Growing up, I observed much fear around me and a constant striving to accumulate wealth, often at the expense of other human beings. It made me realise that there are few soft places to fall in a capitalist society.

So how would you describe your cage? A society which dictates 'survival of the fittest'? A culture where you suppress your feelings and needs in order to make money? A work ethic that leaves no time to sit and stare?

"It's not that bad."

Do you believe that it's your birthright to be joyful? To use every one of your precious days doing something fulfilling?

"Of course I want to be happy. I guess I have learned to live with the boredom and dissatisfaction of everyday life."

There is living and there is making a living.

I ponder the difference for a few moments. She is gently nudging me to examine something I usually ignore. I shift my position on the wooden bench.

Let's start a fresh page in your journal. Write this heading:
Discovering Me

*You need to start questioning everything you know, even the things I share with you. A powerful **secret** is to always ask: Is this true? How can I know this is true? Does this make sense to me? How does it make me feel?*

"Once I start questioning everything, won't I be left in a state of uncertainty?"

Discovering YOU means stripping away the confusing demands, expectations and labels of your parents, society, culture, religion and the media … and looking deep within to find your innate traits, talents and dispositions. Your traits, talents and dispositions are the **keys** *to experiencing lasting happiness and joy. These will be your guiding lights.*

"My innate traits, talents and dispositions?"

Your innate traits, talents and dispositions exist prior to the cage of socialisation. If you cast your mind back, you may remember that you displayed particular patterns of thought, feeling and behaviour early in life. You may have shown a tendency to enjoy your own company more than interacting with others; you may have been energetic and intense while your sibling or friend was naturally quiet and calm; and you may have been drawn to particular interests and activities.

Discovering YOU means finding your unique voice and unique footprint. It's time to discover and unveil your beautiful, sweet centre.

"That sounds rather lovely."

Here is an exercise for you. Imagine you have lived a long and joyful life on this earth, and now you have passed on. What would a newspaper or magazine journalist write about you and your life? How would you be remembered? Write this article in your journal now. I will return in one hour.

Tethys glides away, melting into the expansive blue lake. It feels a bit exciting to be searching for my inner being. My boot thoughtfully swings through the long grasses at the lake edge, then I take a deep breath and begin writing.

* * *

An hour later I am astounded by what I have written. In short: I left the accountancy profession; I created beautiful art which brought joy to others; and I lived near a beach in a warm country. There is no mention of Robert.

The water-goddess forms before me with a gentle purling. Her eyes are compassionate crystals.

"I don't recognise myself, Tethys. Yet deep inside the story feels true. How can this be? Is there –"

A sublime melody interrupts my thoughts. I catch my breath – it's the same tune I heard on Thursday night! Playing a little louder this time. I close my eyes as the enchanting sound engulfs me.

"What is that music? Where is it coming from?"

There is a stillness, and then: *It is the song of your heart.*

I open my eyes wide. "I recognise this. I used to hear it when I was a child. It has been so long ..." A solitary tear rolls down my cheek.

Your Heart Song is the essence of you. This beautiful melody is always playing deep inside your soul.

"I had almost forgotten how it sounds. Where has it been?"

Sometimes the voices of others drown out your Heart Song. Sometimes your life choices move you away from your Heart Song and it begins to fade. When you can no longer hear your Heart Song, no one else can hear it either, and so your life drifts into routine, boredom, sadness, and even depression.

"I can't hear it anymore."

Don't worry, you will. The more you discover you, the more you will hear your Heart Song. Your Heart Song is your true guiding light in this life.

"How can I discover me? What else can I do?" I hear the hurried London tone in my voice.

Be patient. It's enough for now. Close your journal and go for a leisurely walk. Take the time to immerse yourself in nature. Try to be fully present with everything you sense. Learn to be where you are.

She dives into the water, leaving me standing on the shore with more questions than answers. I follow her suggestion and take the long route back to the cottage, fully embracing all the natural sights, scents and sounds, and a wondrous peace comes over me. Two hours disappear in this magical space.

By the time I return I am exhilarated and starving, so I offer to take us out to the local pub for supper. We find a table near the crackling fire and delight in the great ambience and excellent, locally sourced food. I don't feel ready to share the day's experiences and Lilura does not ask.

* * *

I rouse slowly and glance at the clock. Gosh, is that the time? Such a long and restful sleep; so unlike me, and two nights in a row. Perhaps it is the fresh country air. Perhaps it has to do with the water-goddess. I feel invigorated and reconnected on some deep level.

Mmm, coffee is brewing. The wafting aromas of breakfast tempt me out of bed. I grab my dressing gown and head toward the caffeine. My aunt greets me with her usual enthusiasm: "Hey, sleepyhead! Hungry?"

According to mother, Lilura was always the 'different' sister. Whereas Daphne chose to leave The Lakes and make her life in relatively conservative London, Lilura stayed up here, running drumming, ecstatic dance and shamanic journeying workshops, as well as a fortnightly women's empowerment group. Over time she bought mother's share of the cottage. Everyone seemed pleased with the arrangement.

We sit down to a hearty breakfast. The kitchen door is open and I can see that it has been raining, but now the sky is brightening. A chaffinch hops along the grass, displaying its white wing bars and copper rump, pecking hopefully in the ground for grubs.

"I am thinking of taking another walk to the lake. Yesterday was strange and surreal, and I feel like I have much catching up to do. Do you mind if I go alone?"

"Not at all. I will pack you a light lunch. Take as much time as you need. And remember your journal."

The journal. How did she know to make me a journal?

"Lilura, have you met Tethys before? Did she ask you to make me a journal? Did she tell you I was coming to meet her?"

She gazes out the window for a while, then sighs deeply. "Sweetie, so many questions. Tethys is one of the reasons I stayed here at The Lakes, why I never left the family home. Your mother met Tethys too. We both kept journals."

Oh my ... I am completely shaken by this news. I feel confused and betrayed. My conservative mother knew the water-goddess. "Why did mother never mention this important event? How come no one ever told me?"

Lilura places her hand on mine. "It was your mother's decision. She wanted to protect you, give you a normal life. She knew you would meet Tethys when the time was right."

My thoughts are whirling. Mother knew. Why did she push me into a conservative job? Why did she hide the truth from me? From what was she protecting me?

I push back my chair ... a walk will clear my head ... find my backpack ... make some sandwiches ... bottle of water ... give Lilura a hug and mutter "I am not angry with you" ... vaguely hear her say "Put your hand in the water and make three circles" ... and out into the green fields ... I want to cry, I want to be angry ... but I am stupefied ... my world has turned completely on its head.

The air is fresh and calming, the rhythm of my legs relaxing, and the crackle of leaves underfoot soothing. The chirrup of birds seems to echo in my head and the trees are softly whispering: *What are you doing? Where are you going?*

I arrive at the wooden bench and sit for a while. A few ducks hover nearby, awaiting a scattering of bread. Then I make a decision: I need to see where this goes. What did Lilura tell me? Oh yes ... I dip my hand into the lake and make three circles.

Within moments there is a babbling sound and a swirl of water rises up. Tethys is flowing toward me.

* * *

Greetings, Zara, her voice gurgles lyrically. *Did you bring your journal?*

Now that I am less astonished, I am able to appreciate her unusual beauty. Her form is sensual, curvaceous and crystalline, like sunlight sparkling against a blue waterfall.

"Hello, Tethys. Yes, I have my journal. Are we going to explore my Heart Song?"

She instructs me to open my journal to a fresh page, and use this heading: **Traits, Talents and Dispositions – What I Offer**

Deep within are your innate traits, talents and dispositions. These have always been there. As you discover these, so shall your Heart Song be revealed.

And how do you find these **keys** *to your Heart Song? By asking those who love and know you; by taking long walks and reflecting on your essence; by meditating and contemplating; by visiting a qualified psychometric expert who can measure and report your aptitudes and personality traits.*

The **secret** *is to focus on and develop your natural traits, talents and dispositions – what you can offer to the world – instead of worrying about your so-called 'weaknesses'. 'Weakness' is nothing more than a label propagated by various elements of society.*

You need to be investing your time, money and effort into your traits, talents and dispositions so that they can blossom and flourish. Remember, your 'weaknesses' will never become strengths and the world seeks your strengths!

"At my place of work I have an annual performance review and my weaknesses are usually highlighted as 'areas for development'."

Ah, the Well Rounded Fallacy. A waste of precious time and resources. You see that duck walking there? What would it help if I reviewed the duck's ability to climb a tree? Should I tell the duck that it has a 'climbing weakness' and then send it to a tree-climbing seminar? How will the duck feel if it is foolish enough to accept my imposed assessment? Do you think a self-esteem issue might develop?

Clearly, I should invest in helping the duck become the best swimmer and diver it can be, and leave climbing to the squirrel.

"What if I am an entrepreneur running my own business? Surely I have to be good at everything?"

If your talent is to create ideas, ask your partner to handle the selling. If your natural disposition is to connect with people and not with figures, hire an accountant to do your monthly accounts. To cover your 'weak' areas, partner with people who have complementary skills or outsource the work to an expert.

*A **secret** for effective living is to develop a support system for your 'weaknesses', while you invest in and capitalise on your natural traits, talents and dispositions.*

"Society, business and the media are quick to highlight weaknesses."

And those are the very voices drowning out your Heart Song. Your job is to discover your Heart Song and then accept it exactly as it is.

Your joy and happiness and greatest reward will come from fully accepting, loving, nourishing, growing, investing in, celebrating and sharing your sweet and beautiful Heart Song.

Now in your journal make a list of your traits, talents and dispositions. You may need time to consult others. Try to complete this list over the next two weeks.

I stare into the clear blue sky for a while, then raise my pen and jot down a few ideas. If I enjoy interacting with people so much, why do I work with spreadsheets all day? And what happened to my love of painting? I make a note to chat with Lilura and Robert. Maybe I should book a psychometric test when I return to London.

This exercise requires substantial thought and discussion and there's no point rushing it. I will give myself at least two weeks to complete it.

There is more I need to share with you today. Leave enough space to finish the previous exercise then start a new page with this heading:

Intelligences and Passions – What I Love

There are various types of intelligence. To discover your Heart Song, you need to understand and recognise which ones are manifesting in you. These intelligences were first proposed by Dr Howard Gardner and amended by others over time.

Nature Intelligence: Sensitivity with living things and nature; professions include farmer, conservationist, botanist.

Music Intelligence: Capacity to discern, create and reproduce music; professions include musician, singer, composer, DJ, music producer.

Logic-Mathematic Intelligence: Capacity for numbers, logical thinking, problem analysis, pattern detection, scientific reasoning and deduction; professions include scientist, engineer, computer expert, accountant, statistician.

Body Intelligence: Capacity for body movement and control, manual dexterity and physical agility; professions include dancer, craftsperson, sportsperson, masseur, chiropractor, surgeon.

Language Intelligence: Ability to use written and verbal language effectively; professions include writer, lawyer, journalist, trainer, public speaker.

Self Intelligence: Ability to recognise own thoughts and feelings, appreciate the human condition and question life; professions include psychologist, spiritual leader and philosopher.

Social Intelligence: Capacity for understanding and interacting effectively with others; professions include teacher, social worker, actor, politician.

Spatial Intelligence: Capacity for mental imagery, spatial reasoning, image manipulation, graphic and artistic skills; professions include artist, designer, beautician, photographer, sculptor, town planner architect, inventor, engineer.

Note in your journal which intelligences are dominant in you.

How brilliantly useful! I can see myself immediately. I have spatial intelligence, manifested in my artistic abilities; social intelligence, displayed in the way I interact with others; and logic-mathematic intelligence, which I use everyday as an accountant.

The examples of the professions highlight an obvious fact: my dominant intelligences are spatial and social – the very areas I am not using in my daily work. Logic-mathematic is a lesser intelligence, yet that is my profession. No wonder I am so unhappy.

"This is a revelation, albeit an uncomfortable one. And I never realised a journal could be so useful."

*Lastly, you need to list your **Passions**. What do you love? Here are the questions to answer in your journal:*

What would wake me with great anticipation every morning? What secret dreams would I love to do or try? What are my unfulfilled goals? What themes or threads run through my life? What makes me come alive? When do I find myself doing exactly what I want to be doing and never wanting it to end?

Again you may need to ponder and meditate on these questions. Try to complete all of today's exercises over the next three weeks.

I am stunned. What marvellous questions to consider. I put my journal to one side and unpack my lunch. It has turned out to be a splendidly warm autumn day and I want to savour the gorgeous weather. After a long, luscious stretch, I pour a cup of coffee from the flask and gaze across the serene lake.

The crystalline water-goddess leaves me in my reverie for some ⌐⌐kes her body wildly, sending water droplets ⌐ard me. Our eyes hold for a moment and a ⌐quillity falls upon me. "Thank you," I whisper, as ⌐ and flows into the perfectly still lake.

I spend the next hour basking in the delicious sunshine, breathing in the crisp air and soaking up the sounds of nature. I have no desire to do anything and my mind, for once, has quietened. I have many questions but I sense that the answers will reveal themselves in time.

Eventually I make my way to the cottage. Lilura and I enjoy a cup of tea and chat about the day's events, but it looks like she already knows how it unfolded. We share a cheerful hug and I express my gratitude for her generosity and kindness. The journey back to London gives me plenty of time to consider my intelligences and passions.

* * *

The week begins like any other. My morning shot of espresso or cappuccino, warming porridge or raisin toast, run for the bus, nip into the café for a cream cheese bagel to enjoy later, hang up my coat, greet everyone – "yes, I feel much better, thank you", check my diary, scan for urgent emails. The weekend is soon forgotten.

The bus home gives me the opportunity to observe my city. All frenetic activity, smog, noisy traffic and tall buildings, with barely a tree in sight. I sigh. What am I doing this all for? Just to pay the rent? And take an occasional holiday?

I am reminded about Tethys' questions. Perhaps I will update my journal tonight. It will be good to think about what gives me fulfilment and pleasure.

It is a short walk from the bus. The wind is blowing and the chilled air breezes beneath my coat. The blazing vermilion of the tapas bar looks inviting and I really don't feel like cooking tonight, so I am soon ensconced with a glass of house red and a menu. A flyer on the table catches my eye, piquing my interest: Art Classes for Beginners. I stuff it into my handbag.

Later I enjoy a long soak in a hot bath, then grab my journal and head to my wingback chair. Brushing my hair warms my heart and slows my busy thoughts. I start to wonder about the weekend's teachings. There is much to consider and plenty that longs to be written. The short break has also made me reflective about my life in London.

There is a ripple in the mirror and a shimmer of soft blue light. Our greeting is subtle and wordless, the loving connection immediately felt and understood.

You are here to THRIVE, not merely survive. You are here to LIVE.

"I am concerned that it's too late. I am thirty-four years old today. I have invested in my lesser intelligence and talent. I work long hours. My life with Robert is set ..."

Every moment of every day you choose the life you are living. Your future is the result of the choices you make now.

I frown and stare hazily at the ceiling.

If you don't build your house on solid foundations, sooner or later it will come tumbling down.

On that cautionary note, I open my handbag and pull out the flyer. It has been fifteen years since I did any painting. I am probably useless now. I dial the number, hoping it is not too late to call. A friendly voice answers, introducing himself as Dave, and we have a long chat. The art classes run every Wednesday evening, the next series of lessons starts this Wednesday, and not to worry about my skills. I hang up, feeling very apprehensive.

Every great journey starts with a great root of faith and a great cloud of doubt.

I lay back on my fluffy white pillow and close my eyes. What have I done? Chasing youthful dreams at this time of my life! I am immersed in a full-time job, settled in a sensible profession. And then I hear it: the sweet, melodic strains of my Heart Song. I listen for a while, smiling as the soothing sounds simmer around me, calling me to a deeper place and subtly encouraging me to succumb to the fairy dust of dreams.

* * *

My alarm beeps and my eyes open suddenly. Robert will be back tonight. A trace of anxiety courses through me. Should I tell him about Tethys and the weekend? Will he think I am crazy? What could he possibly say? Is it betraying him if I keep it to myself?

I send him a loving text, finishing with 'Shall I prepare dinner tonight?'. He responds 'Yes, please' then adds 'Can't wait to be home. Am bringing your birthday gift'. With that settled, I put the kettle on and prepare for the daily grind.

The day whirls along the usual merry-go-round of pleasing and performing, and by five-thirty it is a relief to be out of the office and shopping for groceries. I will serve one of his favourite meals tonight and then mention the art classes and perhaps a little of the weekend. Hmm ... fillet steak, patatas fritas, corn and a Doña Paulina Merlot, that should do it. I am smiling. Does this fall under social intelligence?

It is lovely to see Robert; we embrace and kiss and I help him unpack. The gorgeous bouquet of red roses slips easily into a vase on the dining room table. Over dinner we discuss his business trip and my wish to commence the art classes. I decide to avoid the weekend's activities. After dessert he hands me my birthday gift. I pull the white ribbon and the little box opens to reveal an ornate, silver charm bracelet with semi-precious stones. I am delighted and give him a big thank-you kiss.

Later I am lying awake, listening to him sleep. Why does it always feel like I am alone in bed? I long for him to hold me, but the only affection comes from the feathery touch of the duvet on my naked body. I close my eyes and imagine laying on a sandy beach, the caress of the sun on my thighs, the whisper of a light breeze, the scent of flowers in my hair. There is a familiar tingle as my hand brushes gently over my tummy. I hear the soft swoosh of sapphire waves tantalising me into a delicious ebb and flow ... gradually immersing me in pleasure ... until I quietly bite my lip ... oh!

* * *

A ripple of anticipation and apprehension: my art class starts this evening! I want the day to disappear so I can get the lesson done; instead it drags interminably. Finally I nip home, eat some chicken salad, then walk the fifteen minutes to the venue.

An assortment of amateurs greets me – housewives, arty types in bohemian clothing, a retired couple, and people rushing in from corporate jobs. Friendly Dave introduces himself and lays down the ground rules. Each student is given the opportunity to say a few words about their experience and aspirations. I start to relax. This is not as scary as I thought. The backgrounds are diverse but we are all pretty much on the same level.

The next few weeks are a blur of colour theory, colour mixing, brushstrokes and paints – oils, acrylics, watercolours and pastels. I prefer acrylics as they dry quickly, mix and clean with water, and allow me to paint out and hide mistakes. We are encouraged to experiment on paper, canvas and board, and I soon learn that each surface has something wonderful to offer.

The classes are moderately challenging and often quite entertaining. I manage to present one decent piece of work after three months and Dave is kind and generous with his feedback.

At the end of six months the basic course finishes. I bring home my second 'masterpiece' and stand it in the hallway. It is a picture of a water-goddess floating serenely on a lake. Robert is admiring it on his way out the door. "It's rather unusual. What inspired you?" I just shrug, smile and kiss him goodbye. Tomorrow I will tell him that I have signed up for the Intermediate Art Class.

Later in the evening I am sitting in my wingback chair, casting a critical eye on my work, when a silver-blue glow from the mirror dances across the room.

"Hello, water-goddess, it's been a while." I smile happily at her.

Hello, Zara. I am appreciating your painting. It's beautiful.

I regale her with the last six months of my life, taking care to express my gratitude for her inspirational teaching. My journal has become a comforting source of guidance.

Are you ready for the next level? You will need a fresh page.

"Yes, of course." I open the bedside drawer and search for a pen.

Write this heading: **Fulfilling My Needs – What I Require**

You previously set out to discover your traits, talents, dispositions, intelligences and passions. This helped you be clear about what you offer and what you love. It also helped you remember who you are and thus awakened your Heart Song.

Now I would like you to start thinking about your **needs**. *What is it you want out of life? What are your relationship and emotional needs? What are your physical and intimacy needs? What are your professional and financial needs? What are your social, community and home needs?*

I raise my eyebrows. "Those are difficult questions."

*Most people never stop to think about their needs. Yet knowing your needs is one of the great **keys** to finding deep fulfilment and joy. How can you build your dream life if you don't know what you need?*

"It feels a bit selfish and self-indulgent to list all my needs."

Is that the sound of other people's voices trying to drown out your Heart Song?

"I have never given serious consideration to my needs. I am so used to pleasing and compromising. I feel a bit apprehensive. Do I have to write all my needs in my journal?"

To create your dream life, you need to MANIFEST your inner world. Your journal takes your inner world and splashes it onto physical reality for you to view. Just as when you are creating a painting.

I fold my arms and gaze into the rippling mirror. "Yes, I understand this ... manifesting my inner world ..."

Take the time to ponder and contemplate, then write as much as comes to you. Use no more than two weeks to complete your list of needs. And remember: these are fluid lists, so you can add to or amend your lists whenever new ideas arise and whenever your inner world evolves.

There is a swirling motion and the mirror settles into its usual solid silver. I go downstairs and return with a cup of tea, then slide cosily into our huge bed. My journal lies open before me, inviting me to explore my inner world and urging me to manifest my Heart Song. I pick up my pen and begin writing ...

* * *

A chaotic year has flown by.

I am faithfully recording and updating my passions and needs. My understanding of myself has deepened and I regularly enjoy wonderful moments of hearing my Heart Song. It comes and goes, sometimes faint and sometimes easily audible. I am noticing a subtle and steady move toward happiness and peace.

Confusingly, my home life is a roller coaster of dissension, friction, strife and arguments. We have been together for three years, sharing a home for the last two. I don't know what's happening. Some days we feel close but other days we are strangers living under the same roof. Where has the joy gone? Is it supposed to be this hard?

Tonight I am graduating from the Intermediate Art Class. I am very pleased to have come this far. Though my first love is painting, this year I discovered the joy of drawing and sketching and now have a bountiful collection of graphite and wax colour pencils, inked brushes, crayons, charcoal and chalk.

I am hoping to be selected for the Advanced Art Class (you cannot automatically progress to this level). This class involves a two-year commitment with two lessons per week as well as dedicated time required for producing high quality painting and drawing. It also offers opportunities for painting vacations.

My only concern is that my home life will be a disruptive influence. Robert is no longer supportive of "the hobby", as he calls it, and pays scant attention to my work. Maybe my increasing happiness bothers him. Perhaps he feels that he is not getting enough of my attention.

Our paths cross on the way to the graduation ceremony. His lips brush my cheek lightly as he grunts a greeting; I whisper a goodbye. A short walk and I am surrounded by warm conversation and focused stillness. This is one of the few places where I feel like I truly belong.

Thirty of us completed the intermediate level; only ten of us will be selected. I hope my submissions pass the test. Did I capture the mood of my subject? Did I use colour, light and contrast in an optimal manner? Will the brushstrokes meet the technical requirements? I hear my name so I jump up and collect my graduation certificate. There is no painting tonight, instead we are celebrating our graduation with drinks and canapés. Letters regarding the selection have been mailed to our homes.

I am studying the notice board in the foyer. The advanced class offers the opportunity to spend two weeks each year on a painting vacation abroad. The first one is only three months away and it's in Loutro, Crete – a little island surrounded by the warm Mediterranean sea, just off the mainland of Greece. My heart leaps. It's in June. Summer in an isolated paradise. Nothing but gorgeous weather, swimming and painting!

Robert is already asleep when I get home. A cup of refreshing tea will comfort my loneliness. Why are our lives drifting apart? I switch on the kettle and open my journal to the section titled 'Fulfilling My Needs'. Reading carefully, I become aware of a disparity between my relationship needs and what Robert seems able to provide. How come I never noticed this before?

My success in art class, and my increasing happiness, has shown me the value of focusing on my dominant intelligences and the value of nurturing my talents. Unfortunately I have been ignoring my needs, so I resolve to start paying more attention to these.

The next day the letter arrives. I have been accepted into the advanced class! I feel jubilant and raise my hands and whoop and dance around the front room. Then I feel a bit dejected – with whom can I share the good news? I walk down to the tapas bar, order a glass of red wine and phone Lilura. She is thrilled and my mood picks up immediately. We have a long chat and she offers me much support and encouragement.

After a couple of drinks I phone Dave. I try to contain my exuberance but it gushes down the line. I thank him profusely for accepting me into the advanced class and express my deep gratitude for his tutorship, then ask if there are still places for the art vacation in Crete, saying that I definitely want to go, would he mind booking me on, and where can I get details of the trip? I catch myself – where is all this coming from? I listen to his response, then wish him a good evening. Maybe I just need to escape home for a while.

* * *

As June approaches the distance between us seems to increase. I make my final arrangements and determine to spend a couple of nights in a spa hotel before catching the direct flight from London Heathrow to Heraklion, Crete. A little pampering, relaxation and a good book will be the perfect transition between a stressful home life and a sunny art vacation.

Robert appears nonchalant about the holiday. "Hope you arty types have a great time," he says coolly over a glass of Chardonnay. He enjoys the tense, vivid palate of a good white wine; me, I'd choose a thrilling blend of Malbec and Cabernet Sauvignon any day of the week. I sigh. Maybe we are quite different after all. He gives me a quick peck on the cheek and says goodbye. I leave the house and a wonderful feeling of relief spills through me.

After a couple of luxurious, self-indulgent days, I join Dave and five students at Heathrow airport. It's all smiles and hugs and buoyant conversation. The plane lands promptly in Heraklion; then we enjoy a long bus ride through the countryside to Sfakia, a little port village. Here we wait in the melting sun for the ferry to Loutro.

When it arrives we clamber aboard and hide under the shade of an awning, enjoying the magnificent Mediterranean seascape and invigorating ocean breeze. Eventually a sprawl of white buildings comes into view. Little boats are scattered near restaurants residing at the water's edge and small rises of white apartments shimmer against a backdrop of stony, arid hills.

The intensely pitched hum of tree crickets greets us as we get closer. One of the students explains that cicadas like heat and do their most spirited singing during the hotter hours of the day. It is difficult to locate the direction of cicada song, as cicadas tend to make their hypnotic noise in unison.

We check into Athitakis Pension. My heart is thrilled when I discover that my top-storey room has a spectacular view of the turquoise sea. I stand on the balcony and admire the gorgeous panorama for a long while, then change into my bikini, grab my towel and head for the beach.

I feel a bit self-conscious in a bikini but I want the sun to lavish its attention over my entire body. I take a deep breath and try to remember that *everyone* is wearing practically nothing. Most of the European men are in skimpy swimwear, while a few others display boxer briefs. It is not long before I am surreptitiously gazing at some of *their* rippling physiques from behind my dark sunglasses.

The shore is all pebbles so I purchase a pair of slip-on beach shoes to walk comfortably into the water. Rounded stones of various sizes layer the sea bed for a few yards out, and the water is an incredible translucent green with great visibility. The sea feels cool and exhilarating as I dive down to look around. I have always loved swimming and adore being underwater. It brings a peace I cannot explain.

In the evening we meet the European students. We have booked a long table at a taverna. Carafes of water, with plates of bread and olive oil, bedeck the white table cloth. Fourteen of us and two art tutors make for a clamorous and fun dinner. We order meze, a variety of small dishes served with wines or anise-flavoured liqueurs. Soon a medley of delectable Greek flavours is tantalising and caressing our palates.

Of the fourteen students, there are two couples who have been together for a long while. Four of us have left our partners to be here. The other six are single, four women and two men. Presumably, then, only two eligible men. I smile at myself – am I calculating the odds on coupling? The nationalities range from English to Greek, French, Italian and Croatian. Fortunately everyone converses comfortably in English.

The only pause in the ebullient conversation is when a blazing yellow sun spreads its cape and dances over the dark blue sea. We raise our glasses and together salute one of the most enchanting sunsets I have ever seen.

Later we enjoy an array of decadent Greek desserts. I gaze along the water's edge at the muted lanterns and bright flower boxes. The cool evening breeze is a gentle blanket on my naked shoulders. A dreamy baklava, with layers of nuts in honey-drenched filo pastry, melts in my mouth. My soul is purring.

* * *

The day starts promptly at eight o'clock in a little cove at the far end of the beach. Dave and Michaela (the tutors) explain that we will paint until midday, then the rest of the day is ours. We will reconvene at seven in the evening for the group dinner at a different restaurant.

We set up our palettes and easels. This week we will be learning how to paint or sketch landscapes and waterscapes. The tutors demonstrate a few specialised techniques and encourage us to experiment with our style. The sun is warm and it is not long before I feel rivulets running down my back and legs. I make a mental note to switch to my bikini and sarong.

There are two of us at this particular spot. Presumably we are both desiring the same vantage point: a charming little alcove of emerald green water. He is a rather quiet man who is studiously focusing on capturing the tranquil sea. His sketch appears to be coming along nicely and I comment in a positive manner.

He does not look up, but half an hour later he gazes at my painting and says, "It lacks passion. Why are you suppressing your fire?"

I don't know what to say. What a cheeky man. I quite like my work so I ignore him and carry on painting. When I look over again just before lunch, I notice he has sketched a sensual female coming out of the water. I want to ask him about this but it is lunchtime, and within minutes he packs everything away and is gone.

Michaela offers a few kind words and everyone gradually drifts off to enjoy the rest of the day. I am still slightly ruffled by the quiet chap's comments and decide to stay alone by the alcove for a while. A tree provides shade from the searing sun and it is peaceful listening to the rippling water.

There is a familiar swirling sound. I look across the sea and there in the distance a shape is forming. Could it be Tethys? I have not seen her for over a year.

Hello, Zara. It is good to see you.

A smile lights up my face. "It is you! Where have you been? What are you doing here?"

She moves closer to the shore and I leap in to give her a squelchy hug. I feel an inexplicable connection with this strange being.

Do you have your journal with you? I have another exercise for you.

"It's in my room but I will remember your instructions."

Use this heading: **Creating My Reality**

Then write this sub-heading: **My Ideal Day**. *I would like you to record the story of your Ideal Day from the time you get up in the morning until the time you go to bed. What is happening? What are you doing? Who are you with?*

Ensure you write in the present tense, describing the day as if it is happening now. Just put pen to paper and write without thinking. Let the words flow naturally, unhindered by self-judgement and self-criticism.

And then she is gone as quickly as she arrived. I decide to leave my easel and paints in the shade of the tree. I nip back to my room, find my journal and insert the required headings. After changing into my bikini and sarong, I stroll to a taverna and order a Greek salad. It is without doubt the tastiest and most refreshing salad I have ever eaten: scrumptious layers of tomato, cucumber, red onion, feta cheese and pitted kalamata olives, all dressed with olive oil.

I rest for a while, sipping plenty of ice-cold water and gazing out over the blue-green sea. A light breeze flutters my hair. A delicious tingly feeling caresses my inner thighs. I suddenly realise I am staring at the lithe body of my arrogant art partner who has erupted from the cool water a few yards away. Water is dripping from his lean, slightly muscular body. I bite my lower lip for a moment.

I turn my head away but it is too late. He is ambling toward me, a warm smile on his lips, his curly, dark hair ruffled by his towel. I open my journal to a blank page and pretend to read. He saunters past my table, oblivious to me, and joins one of the single females. Soon they are giggling over a couple of frosty beers. What an imbecile! I grab my journal and walk to the shaded tree by the alcove.

Opening to the page titled 'My Ideal Day', I relax and allow my thoughts to flow. A torrent of ideas pours out of me and an hour easily disappears. Was I supposed to write this much? I lay my pen down and drink some water. After a few minutes I read my stream-of-consciousness and am astounded. I hardly recognise my life.

It seems my ideal day involves teaching and connecting with others. What were my dominant intelligences again? I page back through my journal then return to the current exercise. In summary: art is my work; my profession connects me with others; teaching and mentoring are central pillars; I am living in a warm climate near a beach; the sea plays a big role in my life; and I am in love with a wonderful man, someone gentle, passionate and stimulating, someone with similar interests, someone with whom I share my life.

I stare at the words I have written. There is no mention of Robert, London or my accountancy job. What does this mean? Is my Heart Song completely disconnected from my real life? Or is it the other way around?

A sudden urge overtakes me. I splurge a frenzy of sparkling oranges and reds in bold brushstrokes across my sedate turquoise painting, creating a smouldering terra firma pushing, erupting, arising –

"Much better. I like it." My quiet partner is standing behind me, his bare chest lightly touching my shoulder. I feel exposed and vulnerable as he analyses my canvassed soul. His warm breath tickles my ear. "This is more you. Beautiful technique, strong message."

I really don't need his opinion. British men are far more polite. I am softly biting my lower lip again.

"Feel like a swim?" he offers playfully. I turn to look at him; his eyes are a curious cyan and his dark curls are dancing just over his ears. He is slightly taller than me, which I like.

Suddenly he picks me up, and I am trying to tell him to put me down, which he does by throwing me into the cool water and jumping in after me. I feel infuriated and shriek and splash at him. "You idiot!" I say, then I am giggling while trying to maintain my don't-mess-with-me face.

He heads toward the deeper water, beckoning me to follow. He is a strong swimmer and we surf the small waves like a pair of dolphins, then dive down and frolic like baby seals in our natural environment. A wonderful serenity settles upon me. It's so beautiful down here.

The swirling movement of a translucent, feminine form distracts us. Maybe ten yards away ... Tethys! I glance over to see his reaction and there is only calm on his face. I surface for a gasp of air then stick my head underwater again; he is still hovering and seems entranced. Moments later he breaks the surface, smiling like a porpoise. I wait for him to speak but he says nothing.

We swim to the shore and stretch out on a warm rock in the shade of a tree. He is laying on his tummy, gazing at me. "I am Xavier, by the way ..." I feign surprise: "Yes of course, I know. And I am –" "Zara," he interjects. I blush slightly, hoping it is invisible on my warm skin. My polite quietness encourages him to begin chatting.

Xavier has a mixed European heritage, a little Greek, a little Italian. He lost his parents early in life through a boating accident. Perhaps this is why he appears to be a drifter, a ship without an anchor. Not the ideal partner for a sensible accountant.

His one passion is 'freediving' which he describes as the sport of breath-hold diving (no tanks). Freediving includes leisure activities such as spearfishing and snorkelling as well as competitive disciplines: Constant Weight, Free Immersion, Variable Weight, No Limits, Dynamic and Static Apnea. He reaches for his phone and explains these by playing a couple of gorgeous underwater videos. Although Xavier no longer competes, he truly loves being underwater. "It is one of the few times I feel absolute peace," he says, smiling at me.

I smile back. "I adore being cocooned by the ocean."

He stretches out in the sun, his olive skin starkly contrasting with my lily-white complexion. "We should go snorkelling some time. That would be fun."

And then he is asleep. I lay staring at the azure sky, little flashbacks of home creeping through my consciousness. Why is my mind always so restless?

Later in the evening we enjoy another group dinner. An interesting mix of lyre, laouto and mandolin enlivens the atmosphere. The warm sun and fresh sea air have lightened my appetite, so I order a small portion of briám: oven-baked ratatouille of summer vegetables on sliced potatoes and zucchini. When it arrives my taste buds dance an ecstatic sousta.

* * *

It's a new day and the sun ripples gold across the water. A couple of transient clouds streak the perfect blue sky. I slip on my beach shoes and stroll to the art lesson. The cicadas are already humming.

My body feels rested and there is a gentle song in my heart. I reach the rocky outcrop at the end of the beach and, to everyone's surprise including my own, I leap into the inviting sea. Moments later I am attending the tutorial with avid attention.

What has come over me this morning? I am painting with reckless abandon, all whizzes and feisty strokes, a blur of deep blues and hazy greens and hints of sparkling white. Michaela gives me a little personal advice, so I add a few surreal touches.

By lunchtime I have completed something wild and spectacular and so unlike me. I stare at the picture for a long while: it is a noiseless, deep, dark underwater scene, at once lifeless yet teeming with unseen power, with something small and crystalline that feels enticing and seductive.

Xavier pads over, peruses the painting in his own quiet way, then says, "I recognise this place. I have been there. Perhaps you will see it with me one day." His brow furrows as he speaks; there is a serious tone in his voice. My curiosity is piqued. Is there something he wants to share with me?

Then Dave arrives and the moment dissolves into painting techniques and jovial small talk. I decide to join him and a few students for lunch. We traipse to the nearest taverna and order pitchers of ice-cold water, warm meze and exquisite Greek salads. The sweet, juicy tomatoes are marvellous – *this* is how tomatoes are supposed to taste!

After some lazy conversation, I fill my water bottle and amble back to the alcove. There are a few questions whirling in the back of my mind and I am hoping that Tethys will make an appearance.

Heat waves are shimmering on the distant ridge and the cicadas are in full swing. A gentle breeze flirts with my sarong as I gaze adoringly at the ocean. The constant unfurling of silver-tipped waves is delightfully entrancing. Eventually I dip my hand into the water and make three circles. Soon a familiar shape forms before me.

You have questions, Zara?

"Thank you for coming. Would you mind if we talked more about **Creating My Reality**?"

Do you know why you are keeping a journal?

"To guide my life? To document the lessons? To record my progress?"

*Your journal helps you discover your Heart Song and splash it onto physical reality. It assists you in **visioning** and manifesting your inner world.*

"Do you mean that I am creating my reality as I write?"

Indeed. As a supplement to your writing, you can also collect pictures of jobs, lifestyles, locations and other inspiration from magazines, newspapers and the internet. Then put these in a Vision Box, like a personalised hatbox, or place them on a Vision Board, a large felt or cork board mounted on a bedroom or study wall. A modern Vision Board could be a photo album in your computer.

"I prefer the last option. It's a great idea."

Autobiographies also impart stimulating ideas and superb lessons. You can read about the journeys of people that inspire you, whether it be a political leader, a wealthy business person, a spiritual teacher or a great artist. What choices did they make? What challenges did they face? What was the cost of the dream?

"Are **choices** and **challenges** the essence of reality creation?"

Every moment of your life is the result of the choices you make. Sometimes your choices may feel very limited. You may be facing seemingly insurmountable challenges. You may be in a situation called No Way Out. This can happen when finances are very tight and you are in the wrong job or in the wrong relationship. It appears that you cannot move.

But we all have choices. We all have a Sphere Of Influence. Sometimes you will only be able to move in tiny, incremental steps to reach a dream. Sometimes you can only change one small thing, then another, then another.

"I am fortunate to be earning a decent salary, although my work is unfulfilling and my romantic life is empty. I need to start in one area, making small changes, one step at a time, at a pace I can emotionally and financially manage."

You need to **accept** *what* **is** *in your life. Then begin to* **change** *what you* **can***, creating steady ripples in your Sphere Of Influence. One of the biggest* **secrets** *of reaching a dream is steadfastness, determination and patience.*

"Oh no! I am not built for patience. I am restless, unhappy and frustrated. I am in my thirties. Time is running out."

A hundred-mile walk is completed step by resolute step. A beautiful house is not built in one day. Both require commitment, dedication and unwavering action.

"Choices and challenges I understand, but **costs**?"

Every choice and every lifestyle has a **price tag***. An ambitious businesswoman may lose her marriage as she climbs the corporate ladder. A political leader may feel quite isolated and alone, with few enduring friendships. The office worker may have a boss he does not like, so he becomes an entrepreneur and finds that he is working extraordinarily long hours. The artist may have to sacrifice financial security as she progresses toward her dream of full-time joyful creativity.*

"Why can't it be easy? Why can't we just manifest our dreams? Breathe it into reality?"

You are doing just that, Zara. However, it is not an instant magic manifestation; rather, it is a process you need to follow. Hence your journal.

Here are the real questions: What is your dream? What is the reality you wish to create? How much do you want it? Are you willing to face the challenges? Are you prepared to pay the price?

If your vision is muddled and your commitment is weak, you will travel in the wrong direction. If your vision is clear and your commitment is strong, you will enter into **flow** *and start to attract synchronicities into your life.*

"It's the price tag that I don't like."

You need to be conscious of the emotional, financial and time costs of working toward your dream. Doing the advanced art class has cost you time. This may have impacted on your home relationship too. These are things you have unconsciously chosen. Now is the time to be mindful of where you are going and what it is going to cost. How much do you want your dream? Will it be worth it?

"Oh, I see." I pause and stroke my chin thoughtfully. "You are awfully pragmatic for a water-goddess."

A soft, gurgling sigh. She casts me a patient stare. *You live on this earth; you are an earth-being. If you are a fire-being, an air-being or a water-being, different rules apply.*

"What are you talking about?"

At a fundamental level you choose your reality. You decided to be an earth-being, so I am teaching you earth-being rules. Come swim with me.

There is mild apprehension as I enter the water and wade out to Tethys. A peculiar sound catches my attention, encouraging me to look over my shoulder. A large wave is forming near the shore and it begins rolling out to sea. I am confused; what I am seeing is not possible. *Hold my hand, Zara!*

The wave engulfs us swiftly, but I am connected to the water-goddess and together we bodysurf with our arms outstretched. The exhilarating swell continually breaks behind us, pushing us further and further until we are surrounded by deep blue ocean.

This is my world. There are different rules for water-beings. Peek underwater.

I am a little scared out here but I take a breath and kick down. Twenty yards beneath me I can make out the shiny crystalline roof of a small building.

Would you like a closer look? I nod with trepidation. *Hold my hand. You won't need to breathe. I will keep you safe.*

I grab her hand and together we glide effortlessly to the shimmering building below. My eyes are wide with shock: I am not breathing; I don't need to breathe!

This is the bell tower of an ancient multi-storey library. Just a few years ago the entire building was completely buried but now it is rising slowly.

I walk through the bell tower with Tethys. The strange crystalline structure is glowing and translucent and solid to the touch. There is no rust nor signs of ageing. I wonder what material was used for its construction.

It's beautiful, isn't it? There are many of these lovely buildings.

There is so much to absorb and so many questions running through my mind. Holding her hand makes me feel like I am part of the ocean. I am solid and free-flowing and it is easy to move through the water. We play around in the ocean for a while then head to the surface. Soon another large wave rises up and we gleefully surf back to Loutro.

About three yards from shore Tethys lets go my hand. My body feels instantly heavy. I stumble out the water and sit by a tree and gaze at the water-goddess. "What a world you live in. What power and grace you possess."

For a moment a solemn look crosses her face. *No one has it all. Life is all about the choices you make. Choose your dream well. Strive for happiness, fulfilment and peace. Think about today's lessons. I bid you farewell.*

I brush the dripping water from my arms and manage a quick goodbye. A light breeze flits over me and clears my head, and I begin to realise one thing: I am never completely surprised by my experiences with Tethys – whether appearing in my mirror or gliding softly in a deep ocean. Something feels so familiar and natural. I laugh softly. What is happening to me?

I walk to the apartment to shower and change; then search for my friends and find them at a stylish taverna on the water's edge. Soon the wine is flowing and I am enjoying hearty Greek fare and warm conversation. Gyros is just what my body needs tonight: meat roasted on a vertically turning spit and served with tzatziki (strained yoghurt mixed with cucumber, tomato, onion, garlic, salt, pepper, olive oil), all on pita bread. Yummy!

A tapping on glass, and in the stillness Dave announces that tomorrow is our day off. I breathe a sigh of relief. A break from the routine and a chance to explore. We order more wine and desserts and the merriment cascades past midnight. I glance coyly at Xavier. I think I know his secret.

* * *

Who is banging on my apartment door? I crawl reluctantly out of bed and look through the peephole. It's Xavier. Great, I can only imagine how I look. I open the door a crack and tell him to go away.

He quickly explains that a boat leaves in one hour to a gorgeous and secluded beach called Sweetwater. Would I like to come, just him and me? I look down and see the picnic basket and the meshed bag of goggles, snorkels and flippers.

I nod and tell him to wait outside. I need a glass of water and a few minutes to pull myself together. About half an hour later I meet him on the steps at the bottom of the apartment block.

"You are very thoughtful," I say. "Why not invite the others?"

"I did but no one wants to go. I guess they have other plans."

"A day out at a secluded beach is just the tonic I need. I am looking forward to doing nothing." I look at the bag and give him a warm smile. "Except swimming, of course. It will be fun snorkelling with you."

He gives my hand an affectionate squeeze, and for a moment our eyes meet and I sense a tingle in my tummy and my heart feels alive. Could something be developing between us?

The small boat arrives and we clamber aboard. There is a bracing sea breeze and the sun is already climbing; it's going to be another spectacular day. Sweetwater beach finally comes into view: a very long strip of white sand nestled between a looming rocky mountain and the greenest sea you can imagine. A few trees line the foot of the mountain, offering a hint of shade. There are probably about fifteen people spread out under rose-coloured sunshades.

We hire an umbrella and loungers and make our way to the far end of the beach. As we pass a few bathers I notice they are completely nude. I have a moment of concern, then Xavier says, "You are allowed to be naked on this beach if you choose. Whatever is comfortable for you."

I don't know whether to laugh or cry. No wonder the art group declined the invitation. My goodness! Doesn't Xavier know about boundaries? Is this a European custom? Or is it a Xavier-free-spirit thing?

"Just so you know, I won't be taking my clothes off. I am not having all these people staring at me."

We settle the loungers under a big tree, taking care to place the water bottles in the shade. Then Xavier strips off and strolls happily to the water. I can't help but gaze upon his fine figure as he walks away.

Moments later he is standing in front of me. "Will you put some sunscreen on my body?" I don't know where to look. I should be polite and turn my head but the desire to take it all in eclipses my manners. I reach for the sunscreen and try to be caring and professional. He quickly adds, "All over, please."

It must be the warm sun that entrances me. Time seems to slow down. I hear the gentle twitter of a bird and the swoosh of waves arriving on the shore. I feel his tanned body under my hands and a wonderful energy courses through my thighs. By the time I am finished we are both smiling.

"Your turn?" he asks kindly.

I hesitate and look around; there is no one within twenty yards of us. Then I do something very unlike me. I slowly undress in front of Xavier. Part of me senses the special energy of this moment and part of me feels a little reckless.

His strong hands apply the lotion gently and gorgeously. Soon I am tingling all over. The sun is soaking into my limbs and a wonderful freedom falls upon me. I push Xavier away, laughing, then run toward the water with him stumbling and giving chase. He tackles me softly just two yards into the sea, and we both crash into the small waves, our bodies tumbling together, the touches creating a sensual charge.

I break free and splash wildly at him. He turns away and shakes his ruffled hair. Then he grabs my waist and we are kissing. I feel his body pressed up against mine as our lips have an intimate conversation. My entire world turns upside down.

We dive into the ocean together and canter along the coast like spirited sea horses. Half an hour later we find ourselves alone in a shallow cove. My heart is racing as he approaches me. Our kisses are intense and passionate, our bodies delirious with desire. Solid rock and shimmering green ... sweet smell of skin ... sensual caresses ... sun whispering liquid honey ... a timeless moment of ecstatic union. Then we collapse giggling onto the sand and lay there awhile, smiling and purring.

The swim back is more leisurely. My heart is warm and full and I have a wonderful feeling of closeness and connectedness.

The afternoon slips easily into bouts of playful swimming, chatting and alfresco dining. I look at this man over some dolmadakia (tasty grapevine leaves stuffed with rice and vegetables). He may not be much of a talker but I feel so comfortable with him; his energy seems to harmonise naturally with me.

On the way back in the boat my mind starts haunting me with questions: Am I one of many women? Is he serious about me? Was that just gorgeous sex? Should I have stayed in my bikini and held the boundaries?

As if sensing my mood, he puts his arm around my shoulder and smiles kindly: "It is what it is, Zara. The soul knows the truth." My heart flutters like a butterfly opening its wings and I kiss him lovingly on the cheek.

* * *

After a light breakfast of yoghurt and honey, I wander over to the art class. Dave and Michaela are giving instruction in brush technique but I find it hard to focus my attention on the teaching. It is a relief when they finally quieten and leave us to get on with painting and sketching.

I need to be alone, so I grab my canvas and bag of art materials and take a stroll past the ferry landing and up the hill, and find a quiet spot overlooking the glimmering emerald water.

There is much to reflect upon. A surreal underwater experience with a water-goddess. A passionate encounter with an interesting and unusual man. A gradual shift into the world of art. I breathe deeply and gaze at the rippling sea. I have no idea where my life is going, but my heart is singing louder than my mind.

I raise my brush and dip into some magenta; it's a great colour and complements the green on my palette. That strange underwater building flashes through my mind as I bite the end of the wooden handle. Then I lower my hand and smoothly apply the first dab of colour.

There is something Zen-like when you become completely focused on an activity. Robert used to say that top athletes get into the 'zone' when competing. I think painting is similar. When I surrender to the creative force inside me and just allow that flow, my sense of time disappears and I find myself immersed in the Here and Now. My sense of self often dissipates at the same time, and is replaced by a beautiful and expansive freedom.

Three hours later I am looking at a magnificent library with marble pillars, crystal ceilings, huge front doors and a lattice of glistening books. It is a most unusual place and I imagine that this is the realm of the water-beings.

The painting needs time to settle; perhaps I will even out the composition tomorrow. Now it is lunchtime, so I move everything back to the apartment and stroll to my favourite taverna. As I approach I notice Xavier sitting alone at a table by the water's edge, staring quietly over the ocean.

I place my arm across his shoulder and kiss his cheek. "Got space for one more?" His face lights up immediately. "Yes, of course." He pulls out my chair and then, "I didn't see you this morning. I was hoping you were alright."

"I needed a bit of alone time, some space to breathe and integrate. How was your morning?"

"My sketch is coming along nicely. I am happy with my work today."

He smiles and his gaze makes my heart skip a beat. What is it with eyes? They convey reams of messages even when the mouth says not a word.

We order the divine Greek salads and our conversation is light and easy. I want to know more about him but I do not want to appear pushy or serious. So we chat about our art and the amazing scenery and the gorgeous weather.

He puts his fork down and wipes his mouth. "Would you like to jump in a kayak with me? We can row to a lovely beach and spend the afternoon. You just need long sleeves and a hat and sunscreen."

"That sounds like fun but I am not very fit."

"It's easy and the pace will be very relaxed. The beach is only half an hour away. See those yellow kayaks? I will rent one and meet you there in fifteen minutes."

I laugh at his sweet exuberance. Twenty minutes later I am appropriately attired and bedecked with a life jacket. Xavier takes the lead position so I can synchronise with his strokes. After turning a few circles I get the hang of it and soon we are serenely cruising across the flat sea. We hug the coastline, which makes me feel secure, and it is not long before a small beach comes into view.

There are about twenty people here, some nude, some in swimwear. We pull the kayak up the beach and disembark like a couple of aliens from a foreign planet. There is a little shop that sells water, cold drinks and snacks. We settle on a warm and cosy part of the beach.

"What exactly do you do, Xavier? How do you earn a living?" I ask, hoping I don't sound rude. He must be in his late thirties and I wish to know a bit of personal history.

"Oh," he sighs deeply, "I studied a degree in architecture and designed buildings for a while. I was never interested in conventional work and got my greatest pleasure when clients gave me free rein to create dreams of chrome and glass. I insisted that my buildings be eco-friendly and sustainable, utilising natural light, recycled rainwater and solar and geothermal heating. People used to say I was a maverick. One day I got tired of battling corporate greed, profiteering and the lack of concern for our planet's welfare."

"And now?"

He shrugs. "I drift here and there. I have worked as a tour guide in Athens; managed a restaurant in Palermo, Italy; served as an instructor in a diving school on the Florida Keys; and sailed yachts across the world for clients. I am no longer chasing money or prestige; now I am searching for my passion, my pleasure."

"You seek the song of your heart." I smile across at him.

"Exactly. That is a beautiful way to say it."

"I wonder if we are all drifting along, seeking our passion and pleasure. Do you think this connects us to our destiny?"

We are laying on our backs staring into an azure sky. He reaches over and places his warm hand on mine. "The more you explore and discover who you are, the closer you come to manifesting your destiny. Destiny is nothing more than the radiance of your soul's unique light."

I blink slowly. Is this what Tethys has been saying all along? Her words swirl into my consciousness: *Your Heart Song is the essence of you. This beautiful melody is always playing deep inside your soul.*

"Have you met the water-goddess?" I blurt out without thinking.

"I have seen her many times, although mostly at a distance. She often appeared when I was freediving deep underwater. Other divers rejected my story as an oxygen-deprived hallucination. However, I believe she is a protective spirit who holds a key to my destiny."

Lying here on this rough sandy beach, the warm sun soaking into me, I realise that Xavier is no stranger after all. I wonder if he feels the same way. I wonder if he is part of my destiny.

The current is with us on the way back so we glide along easily in the kayak. I am watching the twilight reflecting off his shoulders as he rows. The sea gently ripples around us, making soft, soothing sounds. Dozens of tiny luminescent fish leap regularly out of the water, creating rainbow signals to light our way home.

After a long, hot shower we meet for dinner at a romantic taverna. Xavier welcomes me with a loving kiss and a small bouquet of flowers. We are both quite hungry so we order souvlaki (small pieces of meat and vegetables grilled on skewers and served with fried potatoes). Our animated discussion fades gradually into replete stillness and it is not long before we share a nightcap and retire to our own apartments. Sleep will come easy for me tonight.

* * *

I am settling into the ebb and flow of beautiful sunshine, fresh sea air, great food, warm conversation and bouts of fun creativity. For the first time in many years I am sensing a happiness in me and a smattering of peace. I am beginning to think that Xavier is more than a holiday romance, and hoping that something rather special is revealing itself.

I spend the morning refining my crystal-library painting, then pack water and sandwiches into a backpack and wander over the top of the hill. The day is very hot but I am keeping cool in a white cotton dress and sunhat. There are a few old buildings and interesting ruins along the way, and after forty-five minutes I discover a large rock pool along the shoreline.

It must be the effect of the last few days: I ensure that I am alone then strip off and jump into the crisp refreshing water. Ah, bliss – naked and free. I swim around for a while then climb back onto the rocks, lay on my towel and let the baking sun dry me.

It is the bubbling noise I hear first, followed by a familiar eddy forming in the water below. The sea rises up and Tethys is floating a couple of yards from me. There is so much I want to ask her.

"Hello, beautiful water-goddess."

Hello, Zara. Did you bring your journal?

Oh, another lesson. More pointers on the path to my destiny. I need to be positive and go with it. "Yes, it's in my backpack."

We are still in the section called **Creating My Reality**. *How is your vision coming along? Is your dream becoming clearer?*

"Yes, it is. Strangely, the more clear I am about my dream, the more I am attracting elements of the dream to me."

Indeed. Clarity of vision moves you into flow. What is inside is reflected outside. Your heart and mind are busy manifesting in physical reality.

Write this sub-heading in your journal: **Consensual Reality**

There is much talk in your world about attraction, about manifesting your dreams. Some say you simply set your intention and place an order with the universe. However, this ignores the fact the every being is setting an intention at every moment and not all intentions align.

"Every being is setting an intention?"

From the moment you wake up, you set intentions: breakfast, getting to work on time, earning praise for a project, trying for a promotion, looking for love, and so on. Most of your intentions start off consciously then drift into automated mode – they drive you without you having to think. You also have unconscious intentions from your various past experiences.

In a world of seven billion people, with every individual putting out a range of conscious and unconscious intentions, what do you think happens?

"Um … you can find your intentions swallowed up?"

Imagine twenty people are vying for the same job as you. You are competing with those intentions. Some people might even have negative intentions, for example, a desire to harm your reputation.

Tell me: A famished child in Africa, how strong is the child's intention to get food?

"Enormous. Far greater than my intention to get a promotion."

Yet almost one billion people around the world are starving.

"So personal intention is not enough?"

Personal intention is vital but you are enmeshed with the intentions of everyone. Your reality is built by seven billion souls. That is Consensual Reality.

Do you think your world has to be burdened with starvation, war, disease, poverty, wealth disparity and suffering?

"How do I change my life? How can I make a difference in this world?"

By connecting with earth-beings who have similar visions and intentions. You are not meant to stand alone. If you wish to change your personal reality or your earth reality, you have to learn to work together. You need to synergise your intentions and collaborate to create a new consensual reality.

The idea of 'I' is the downfall of most people. There is great power in 'We'. Find beings with similar values, work out a common vision and take action together. This is one the great **secrets** *of successful living.*

The energy around me feels surreal and calm. The rhythmic swoosh of the ocean mingles with the fiery choir of the cicadas. A soft breeze teases my hair as the warm sun sprinkles across my back. I open my flask and sip the ice-cold water, then start making copious notes.

Half an hour later I glance up. She is swaying to a silent melody and scattering rainbow droplets across the rocks. The wise goddess of the ocean smiles at me.

"Tethys, who is Xavier?"

The more you discover and express yourself, the more you will hear your Heart Song, and the more you will attract the right love into your life.

"Is there something else I should be doing?"

All will become clear in time. Your journey is taking a natural progression. Celebrate what's happening now.

And then she is gone, merging into the viridescent water. The sun will set in an hour so I dress and walk slowly back. It gives me plenty of time to consider the lesson of the day. I need to trust the flow, be patient and appreciate what has changed for me.

This evening the entire group is dining together and it's fun regaling each other with vacation anecdotes. On the surface, I am having a great time and the conversations are amusing and entertaining; underneath, my heart is processing and integrating the teachings of the water-goddess.

Later the sound of the Mediterranean lulls me into a luscious sleep.

* * *

Over the next two days I manage to perfect my crystal-library painting and earn solid praise from both tutors. Xavier and I spend time contentedly relaxing on the beach and playing in the sea. We have not made love again but perhaps we both need time to think about what is happening between us. We join the group for dinner but sleep apart every night.

There are only three more days on this island paradise and I am deeply reluctant to leave. I am beginning to taste my dream life and the thought of returning to London fills me with trepidation.

In this morning's art class I get the quaint idea to sketch Xavier while he works on his own project, but my mind is everywhere, and by lunchtime my sketch lies crumpled on the ground.

I ask him if we can go somewhere and talk. Our favourite taverna allows takeaway Greek salads and the owner kindly lends us proper plates with cutlery. We find a lovely isolated spot near the water's edge and perch on the rocks with our feet dangling in the sea. I adore these Greek lunches and it is one of many things I will miss. After lunch we sit staring at the water, while I contemplate my life and future.

"I know we have only just met ... and we have shared some heavenly moments." I pause, trying to select the right words. "You are probably more of a free spirit than I am ... and you are still searching for your Heart Song." I close my eyes for a moment. Come on, say it. "I have feelings for you. Is there something developing between us?"

He continues to gaze into the water. All I can hear is the incessant song of the cicadas. I try not to panic. Have I been foolish? Should I have treated this as a holiday romance and walked away?

Eventually he looks up. "You are a kindred spirit. I sensed it from the first day. I feel happy and peaceful when you are near."

Relief floods through me. I hug him and hold him tight for a few moments. "What can we do? Where do we go from here? I am flying back to London."

"I don't know. I am booked to sail a couple of yachts to Florida and I am short-listed for work on a cruise ship."

What was it that Tethys said? A common vision and a shared dream. "Are you more clear about your passion and pleasure?"

He is quiet for a while. "I know that I love the ocean. I care deeply about the planet. I enjoy diving and sailing. I guess it is not very clear yet. Do you know your dream?"

"I need a warm climate, people, relationships, art and the sea. Perhaps my vision is still a little blurry."

I feel a bit desperate. What use are all the lessons Tethys has shared? Am I going too fast? Am I disturbing the natural progression of things?

We sit in silence. The water gurgles gently beneath us.

The short cough startles me. It's Dave. He asks if he is disturbing us, and may he have a quiet word with me? I invite him over and assure him that he can talk openly in front of both of us. He sits down on the rock.

"It's about your work. Michaela and I have been discussing it. You have made excellent progress in your painting and we have noticed your mentoring skill with the other art students. We feel you have the right qualities to be a tutor. I just thought I would mention it, as the basic art class in London will be expanding and a tutor will be required."

I am momentarily speechless. Xavier claps his hands together: "That's great news!"

"What a wonderful offer. Thank you so much for thinking of me. It deserves serious consideration." I give Dave a spontaneous hug.

"If you would like to talk about the position over the next few days –"

"Yes, yes, of course. I will think of questions. It will be good to discuss."

"Ok, I need to get back to Michaela. Perhaps we will see you at dinner tonight. Enjoy your afternoon in the sun."

Dave wanders off, leaving us alone on the rocks. Xavier looks very pleased. "It's a great opportunity. I am not sure how it helps us connect but it feels right for you."

"Yes, it certainly does." I am a little confused. Is this the flow that results from a vision?

There is a stirring in the water. Soft silver ripples gently draw our attention. We cannot see her but we hear the friendly voice.

Go to the shop and buy a postcard. Sit quietly and imagine it is two years in the future. You are two years in the future. Write yourself a postcard from that time, describing what you are doing and what you love about it. Use a page in your journal if you need more space. Do this exercise within the next two days.

Xavier looks at me. "I'll do mine tomorrow. Let's try to enjoy the precious time we have together." He moves closer and places his arm around my shoulder and kisses me deeply. My stomach tingles.

We spend the rest of the afternoon kissing and chatting and frolicking in the water. Both of us seem truly happy. In the evening we join the rest of the group; it seems the polite thing to do.

Later I am sitting alone on my bed. I decide against buying a postcard. Instead, I put a heading in my journal – **Postcard From The Future** – and start to imagine that I am living two years ahead in time. I let myself drift and start to notice what I am seeing and hearing around me. Where am I? What am I doing with my life? What do I love about it?

It is a simple exercise and I find myself writing far more than expected. I fall asleep holding my journal close to my chest.

* * *

I wake up determined to savour every moment of my time in Loutro. Throwing open the shutters, I gaze fondly over the tavernes, small boats and the sun reflecting off the green-blue waters.

The idea of a cool morning swim entices me and after twenty minutes I am shivering in the crisp air. Wrapped in my fluffy towel, I glance around. Loutro is a tiny seaside resort nestled in the embrace of a steep cliff that towers about six hundred yards above the village. All the apartments and tavernes are white with blue shutters and are scattered alongside an ever-calm turquoise sea.

Amazingly there is no road to Loutro; you can only get here by using the scheduled ferry service from Sfakia or by taking the long coastal walk. There is also no road in Loutro and therefore no cars. It is wonderfully tranquil and feels far removed from the hustle and bustle of modern life.

I am beginning to appreciate Lilura's decision to stay at The Lakes, a setting that is peaceful and nurturing. What is the use of money if not to fund a healthier lifestyle? I am afraid that I have been a victim of consumerism, throwing my hard-earned salary into entertainment, clothing, restaurants and possessions. My home is littered with pretty things that I have bought on impulse. I need to let things go, simplify my life and start focusing on what really counts.

Perhaps I have squandered money in an attempt to fill the emptiness inside me. Is this what happens when we cannot hear our Heart Song? When we don't do what we love for a living? While we are seeking the right romantic partner?

A stream of shimmering wavelets interrupts my thoughts. I cannot see Tethys but I know it is her. Fortunately I have my journal with me.

A final lesson for **Creating My Reality**. *As you discover and blend your traits, talents, dispositions, intelligences, passions and needs –*

begin to consider how these will add value to the world. Adding value to the world is how you generate cash flow to take care of your basic necessities. A healthy cash flow also allows you to fund more dreams and help others.

Write a sub-heading: **How Does My Vision Add Value?**

Ponder this issue over the next few weeks. Talk to family, friends and astute business people. Do research on the internet. Ask these questions:

How does my dream contribute to society and my community? Does my vision solve a problem? Does it offer a valuable service? Is there anything unique or special about my idea? How will my dream better the lives of others? How do I commercialise my vision and earn money?

Remember, you may have to start small. Your passion might begin as a hobby, much like your art. You may have to take a low-paying job to do what you love. You may have to work two jobs. You may decide to start a part-time business, while keeping your full-time job for security and cash flow.

"Thank you for those pragmatic and wise words."

Do what is necessary ... then do what is possible ... and slowly you discover that you are manifesting your dream.

The wavelets subside, leaving me alone with a dozen thoughts. I look at the time; it's already eight o'clock. I scramble to the art lesson. A potential art tutor really shouldn't be late. Xavier raises his eyebrow when I arrive and then smiles in a heartfelt way.

Ok, take a deep breath ... slow down ... locate my sketchpad ... sense the glimmer of sun on my face ... appreciate the expansive sky and those little clouds ... breathe again ... stretch my arms ... notice the soft murmur of the ocean ... breathe ... let go ...

Hmm, a seductive drawing of two lovers intertwined. Yes, that's it. I lay down a broad heart-shape then interpose a man and woman using luscious brushstrokes. I surrender into my creative space, my mind flitting between sweet memories and vivid imagination.

By late morning something wonderful is materialising. The lovers are abstract enough so that neither Xavier nor I can be recognised. But I know and he will know. I intend to make this a portrayal of our time together, a memento of our love affair in Loutro.

After a hasty lunch I spend another hour perfecting the sketch. Then I nip to the shop to find a card and some ribbon. Satisfied, I stash it away in my apartment and go look for Xavier. I feel the time here slipping away.

He is on the main beach and I run over and give him a big hug. The cool sea is a perfect counterpoint to the fiery sun. We swim and laugh and play, knowing all the while that a heartbreaking goodbye is looming.

In the evening we have much to share and celebrate with the festive group. We have all learned so much, not just from the tutors but from each other. It's amazing what you absorb from perusing the various paintings and what you glean from discussions. There is a toast to Dave and Michaela, a thanks for their time and tutelage.

Much later, Xavier and I excuse ourselves and head to the beach. The moon is riding high and draping her soft silver cloak over the water. It is a warm and airless night. We sit on deck chairs and clink our glasses together in gratitude.

He is gazing into my eyes and smiling. I bite my lip. I have no idea if I will ever see this beautiful man again. This precious moment is all we have. I grab his hand and we walk to the alcove.

I want to say so much. There is a warm ache in my heart as he wordlessly sweeps his fingers through my hair. We kiss with mixed emotions, then throw our clothes aside and make glorious love in the balmy air, the stars twinkling across our bodies, the ocean spraying our souls, the moon gently seducing our hearts into ecstatic union.

Two soft rabbits cuddled close under the purple sky, we fall asleep until the morning light gently nuzzles our eyelids.

After breakfast I give my rolled up sketch and card to Xavier, telling him to open them when I am gone. Then it is all packing and showering and we are on the ferry back to Sfakia. Holding hands, we watch as beautiful Loutro slowly recedes into the distance. I sigh. Must all good things come to an end?

We are sitting in the airport counting the minutes. I am feeling a bit tearful. Xavier takes out his postcard. "I want you to have this. My email address is on the back." He gives me a warm hug and then it's goodbye.

The rest of the journey is a blur of heartache, tears and trepidation. My only consolation is that I am returning to an English summer.

* * *

Arriving home is a complete let-down. Robert is waiting at the airport, looking prim in his beige corduroy trousers and dark blue jacket. He appears pleased to see me and I feign a smile. He asks me about the vacation and says he missed me. We chatter away in an apparently comfortable and carefree manner, but deep inside I feel the churning of disinterest, guilt, worry and longing.

The return to work is no easier. Gone are the luscious days painting in the sunshine. No more doing what I love. Surrounded by people who don't really fit with me. The uneasy sense of not belonging creeping back.

The next two weeks are depressing and disappointing, the only respite being the resumption of art classes.

What is the matter with me? I have a good job and earn decent money. I should be grateful and get on with living. I am unlikely to ever see Xavier again – he is probably philandering on various adventures around the world. I don't even know if he genuinely cares for me.

Perhaps I need to put the vacation aside, forget about all those wonderful memories and feelings, and accept my life as it is. I share a home with a good man and have stability and security. Together we enjoy wonderful walks in the English countryside and great theatre and ballets in the city. Maybe Xavier was a silly, impassioned fling.

Unfortunately all our friends are couples so I cannot talk to anyone without the risk of whispers. I have to bury this beautiful secret and try to get on with an ordinary life. I also need to decide about the art tutoring, something I dread discussing with Robert.

At the art class I have a long chat with Dave. The advanced class already requires two evenings per week, as well as practise time on weekends. Tutoring the basic class will cost another evening per week. I will be out of the house Monday, Wednesday and Thursday evenings. There is not much money in tutoring but Dave reminds me of the invaluable experience one can gain from teaching: the joy of mentoring others, the development of people skills, and the subtle refining of artistic talent.

The evening is mild and the sky is still light as I wander home. Dave has sold me on the tutoring idea and I have accepted his offer. He must see some potential in me, so I am remaining open to all possibilities.

Robert is waiting for me in the front room. He smiles warmly as he pours two glasses of Pinot Noir. I glance at the bottle: Cape Chamonix, South Africa. We sit together on the cosy sofa. The window is open and it feels lovely and fresh. I swirl the wine and breathe in the fragrant aroma.

"I have good news, my darling. I had been reluctant to mention some recent business setbacks for fear of upsetting you. Contracts not being renewed, and so on. However, last week I won a lucrative training contract. It means everything is back to normal and the stress I have been under is gone. I realise that I have been moody and distant over the last few weeks and I apologise for this."

There is a pause as he furrows his brow and clears his throat.

"I love you and you mean a lot to me. You being away made me think about our relationship. We have been living together for two years and I was wondering what your thoughts are about marriage."

I am stunned and hold tightly onto my glass. "Robert, this is so unexpected. I don't know what to say."

His voice is soothing and kind. "There is no rush. I am just putting it out there. Perhaps we can talk about it sometime. How was the art class?"

Trembling a little, I answer, "Very good. I am loving it." I take a deep breath. "There is something I should have told you too. During the holiday, Dave and Michaela mentioned the idea of me doing some tutoring for the basic art class. Dave made me a formal offer tonight but it will cost another evening per week. I was not sure of your reaction."

Robert beams a huge smile at me. "That is fabulous news! Well done. He must have spotted some talent. I will be travelling more with this new training contract so you will have plenty of time to master your new position."

I give him a big hug. "Thank you for being so supportive. I am not sure where this art hobby is going but I want to pursue these opportunities."

"Sweetheart, why don't you consider a short diploma in coaching and mentoring? It could boost your confidence and give you some useful skills to employ in art tutoring. You're bright and you could probably do it over a few weekends."

"Where would I find the time? What about us?"

He places his hand gently on my knee. "If you have a dream, you have to be willing to pay the price that comes with it. I will support you. We can make it together."

I feel confused by his words. Have I misjudged him? Has my mother's passing left me in an emotionally dishevelled state? Was it stress that made him seem distant? I look down at the coffee table. There is a neatly bound presentation with dark capital letters running vertically down the cover: **V I K A R**.

"What's that?" I ask, hoping to shift the conversation to more neutral territory.

"Oh, it's the new leadership seminar I am presenting. It is complete *sans* a few tweaks here and there. You are welcome to look over it."

I manage to move the discussion onto his business plans. We finish the bottle of Pinot Noir while he shares several of his ideas. The evening disappears and when we finally retire to the bedroom I am grateful to fall asleep rather quickly.

* * *

It is the end of a long and bewildering week. I open my journal and peruse the lessons of the water-goddess: discovering me, traits, talents, dispositions, intelligences, passions, needs, creating my reality, consensual reality, adding value, visioning and dreaming. What do I do now? Where to from here?

There is a ripple of silver across the mirror. I close my eyes and flop wearily onto the bed. "Are you there, Tethys? I need to know more about my Heart Song."

Your Heart Song is the essence of you. It manifests in those moments when you are truly expressing you.

I cast my mind back. That elegant sound permeated most of my painting sessions ... swimming in the Mediterranean ... the beautiful time I shared with Xavier ... when Dave spoke to me about tutoring ...

"Is the Heart Song only experienced through hearing?"

The Heart Song may be experienced as an exquisite melody, as a magical feeling in your heart, as a mystical shiver along your spine, or as an intuitive knowing in your soul.

There is a fading whisper: *Find Robert's presentation.*

What presentation? Then I recall the VIKAR folder. I go downstairs to the front room and locate it on the coffee table. Well, he did say I could have a look at it. I wonder what Robert could possibly teach me. He is a management consultant; what does he know about art and tutoring?

Back in the bedroom, I put on my reading light and stack some pillows against the headboard. I gaze at the bland white cover with thick black letters: **V I K A R**.

It appears to be a typical, colourless corporate presentation. However, the first page jumps out at me:

V   =   Vision

I   =   Intention

K   =   Knowledge

A   =   Action

R   =   Results

My interest is piqued and I begin to read the rough draft:

'VIKAR is a system to generate shifts in personal, professional and business contexts.

'Creating change starts with producing a crystal clear **vision** after much introspection, soul-searching, self-understanding and discussion. This may be supplemented by psychometric tests, e.g. aptitude, skill and personality measurements.

'**Intention** is the energy you put into the vision. It is the crystallisation of wish and desire. It is the focusing of the mind and energy onto a particular dream. Once you are clear about what you want and you focus your energy, you naturally gravitate toward the appropriate people, circumstances and events.'

In my world we call that 'flow'. You are the creator of flow. When you are in the flow, you feel peaceful; you sense that you are on the right path.

"Thanks, Tethys."

'The crucial starting point is your vision and intention. Without this solid foundation, nothing further will happen.

'However, the real work begins with the next three steps. Once your vision is clear and your intention is invested, you need to collect **knowledge**. If it is a business, you need to learn about marketing, unique selling points, products, reliability, service, cash flow, and so on. If you want to become a therapist, you need to decide which qualifications to study, whether to work at home or hire a room in a centre, how much to charge, and so forth.

'Collecting knowledge may initially take a few weeks, but learning is also ongoing. As long as your dream moves and evolves, you will have to keep adapting and learning.

'**Action** is the application of knowledge.

'The only way to discover what works and what does not work is by applying knowledge. All ideas and theories stand or fall in the wake of rigorous testing in real life situations.

'**Results** refer to the consequences of your actions. Results are the ultimate learning tool. Every result is useful as it gives you feedback and direction. An aeroplane pilot makes numerous minor flight adjustments in order to reach the destination.'

The **secret** *is to not feel defeated when you experience an unpleasant result. Simply say to yourself: "I am learning something. I will try something different."*

'Knowledge–Action–Results creates a valuable **learning cycle**. An unhelpful result indicates that you need to collect more knowledge and/or take different action. You keep learning, keep applying the knowledge and keep observing the results.

'You only reach a dream or fulfil a vision through determined and gradual action over time. Through learning, application, feedback and adjustment. Through ignoring the word 'failure' and by not taking results personally.'

The rest of the presentation is too dry and corporate for my taste, so I close the folder and rest my eyes awhile.

By the time Robert gets in, I am fast asleep. My dreams are a jumble of boats, sunset beaches, palettes of dazzling colour, and a group of enchanted students sitting cross-legged on the sand.

* * *

I awaken slowly on Saturday morning. Robert is already up with coffee and a crisp newspaper. I join him at the kitchen table. "Feel like a cooked breakfast?" he asks, indicating the smoked bacon and organic eggs on the counter. "Yes, please." I smile appreciatively.

It is not long before I am enjoying scrambled eggs, bacon, mushrooms, fresh orange juice, coffee and marmalade toast. We trade sections of the paper, and the silence is interspersed with remarks about political and social events. We debate about a couple of interesting ballets in the review section.

I am looking at Robert over the rim of my coffee mug. He is a lovely man, not very passionate but kind and caring. We enjoy a few similar interests, are intellectually well matched and have a great bunch of friends. We share a three-bedroom house in a decent area; I always feel safe walking down the street.

It makes me wonder. What is it that makes a couple good together? I recently read a carefully researched book that destroyed the myth of 'opposites attract'. In fact, most relationship books emphasise the need for similarity with your partner.

It seems that common interests, values and beliefs are essential in the long run. This may be true. Experience has taught me that 'handsome' and 'sexy' are short term solutions and usually don't sustain a relationship.

I remember the words of Tethys in Loutro: *The more you discover and express yourself, the more you will hear your Heart Song, and the more you will attract the right love into your life.*

"You seem to be far away." Robert is smiling kindly, gazing at me over his reading glasses. I look out the window and sigh. "Just thinking about my life. I skimmed through your presentation last night. It is very good."

"Ah, yes, still a work in progress but the ideas are solid."

"Perhaps I need to sit down this morning and sketch out my vision. A number of ideas have been forming over recent months. If I can draw all the elements together it might create a clear vision to guide my intention and actions."

"Beautifully spoken. I might borrow those words for my seminar."

There is nothing like a long, hot shower to start the day. Afterward I slip into some comfortable clothes and find my journal. I am determined to do this properly.

I glance through the exercises, taking extra time at the 'Postcard From The Future' section. It is all a lot better formed than I expected.

I will write **My Vision** in the present tense, as if it is happening now.

'I am an art tutor. I teach art at a basic and intermediate level. I live near a beach in a warm climate. I am romantically involved with a person who is similar to me and who thrives on affection, loving-kindness, connection and passion. We have a little house and enough money to live comfortably. I am pregnant with our first child. We are very, very happy.'

I close my eyes and vividly picture this reality. I sense the lovely bump in my tummy and the soft touch of the man I love, hear the voices of my students, and notice the easels and pallets scattered along a gorgeous beach. I float in my dream for about fifteen minutes. When I open my eyes, I have a wonderful sense of **intention**, flow and destiny.

What **knowledge** is required for my vision? What do I need to learn in order to move toward my dream? How much will it cost? Is there a price tag? Do I have enough time?

I go online and search for diplomas and certificates in coaching and mentoring. I am working full-time. Monday, Wednesday and Thursday evenings are devoted to the art classes. After a long while I find an accredited and impressive coaching course which can be completed over a number of weekends. A quick calculation: I started the two-year advanced art class in April so there is another twenty-one months to go. The coaching course takes six months, running July to December.

I nip downstairs to discuss it with Robert. He is in his study, doodling absently on a pad of paper. I cough softly, then ask if we can talk about the **actions** I need to take to achieve my dream. To my surprise he is completely supportive, even offering suggestions to handle the time pressures.

My heart feels warm. Things have been difficult between us over the last few months but perhaps I am partly to blame. I give him a big kiss and propose a walk in Hyde Park followed by hot chocolate. He agrees immediately.

We sit by the lake for a long time, watching people walking their dogs, pushing prams, playing casual cricket and idling in the sun. We reminisce about the wonderful music concerts we have watched in the park.

Later we are walking along one of the many tree-lined paths and Robert slips his hand into mine. It feels good, and I respond readily when he kisses me softly under the upside-down tree.

I wonder if I am the only woman to have such mixed feelings in a relationship. He is being so sweet and it is lovely sharing his company. We drift into a café and order hot chocolate and cake. I like mine decadently covered in mounds of cream with little pink marshmallows; he likes his with just a pinch of cocoa.

In the evening we cosy together on the sofa with lamb steaks, chips and salad. We open a bottle of wine and search for a good film on television. Just before bed, I make a mental note to sign up for the coaching course tomorrow.

* * *

Sunday mornings are the best. The sun is twinkling through the curtains but my eyelids are still softly embracing. Robert is moving around the house and I pull the duvet over my head and snooze for a bit longer.

I finally stretch and stare at the ceiling. Today is the one day I can throw colours at a canvas and push the parameters of painting. I smile to myself. It's not Greece but it will do.

After a quick breakfast of granola and soya milk, I nip onto the computer, take a deep breath and press the buy button for the coaching course. Phew, that's it. I am committed. There is a moment of anxiety but then I am off to the garage to paint.

Robert has converted the third bedroom into a study and I have taken over the lengthy garage and made it into a workshop and gallery. It's big enough for two cars parked end to end which makes it an ideal size. At times like this I realise how great it is at home. We have a good partnership.

I put on a long cotton overcoat and find a pallet. Soon peacock colours are flying onto a large stretched canvas. It is a wonderful fabric that has a soft 'give' to it, subtly blurring the boundary between the painter and the painting. Robert pops in once to lavish some praise and later delivers a huge bowl of butter-toffee popcorn with a cup of tea.

Time disappears as I lose myself in my creation. Every so often I become aware of a delicate shift of energy, a magical moment when a joyful melody fills the air. It is my Heart Song. Right now I am doing what I truly love. I sigh happily. Perhaps this is what the water-goddess has been alluding to all along.

* * *

The next six months are a blur of teaching the basic art class every Wednesday evening, attending the advanced classes on Monday and Thursday evenings, practising my art on Sundays, working my way through the coaching course over a number of weekends, completing the coaching assignments, and holding down my full-time accountancy job.

Financially I can manage it, but there is a lot of time pressure. This must be the price tag Tethys spoke about. I realise now that nothing is free; if you want your dream intensely enough, you have to do whatever it takes. Visioning is one thing but it requires courage and diligence to acquire knowledge and take action.

The emotional support from Robert and our close friends helps immensely. We somehow manage to keep our social relationships alive during these busy months and even find time to attend a couple of ballets.

I have had to put Xavier out of my mind. He is undoubtedly cruising around the world having a great time. I am unsure about the events in Loutro, and guilt encourages me to focus on my current relationship. I am learning to truly appreciate my life in London.

When December finally arrives I am relieved and proud to complete the coaching course. The graduation ceremony is a simple affair and afterward we celebrate with champagne cocktails and dinner at a lovely seafood restaurant.

Robert has kindly booked us a week away over the holiday period. It will be a wonderful opportunity to unwind and get to know each other again. I am looking forward to being ensconced in a lovely cottage in Pembrokeshire, just a short distance from Little Haven beach. We can walk the wonderful coastal paths which have expansive ocean views, ride horses through the wooded valleys, and relax in the quaint pubs and restaurants. The perfect respite from a challenging year.

* * *

The new year arrives and along with it a flurry of snow. Many of the minor roads are impassable and I am thankful to be cocooned in our warm house. The fire is crackling and a slow casserole is doing its magic in the oven.

Robert makes a foray to the local shop and returns with a newspaper, popcorn, marshmallows and cocoa powder – mandatory supplies for a snowed-in couple. We surf the television channels for something to watch, then settle for splitting the paper and sipping hot chocolate.

A few days being cosily housebound offers wonderful opportunities. The garage is heated so I spend time pottering with my art, while he surfs the internet and tidies up a couple of seminars. Is this how it is for most couples? Getting on comfortably and easily but without much passion?

During the middle of January things return to normal. Robert's business has taken off and he is away from home at least three nights per week. This leaves me plenty of time to focus on my dreams and vision.

The coaching course seems to have boosted my confidence. Dave is also kindly mentoring me and we sit down once a month for a feedback session. I am slowly discovering the ideal blend of teaching, demonstrating and listening. Students enjoy a combination of space and attention, firmness and kindness, so I am learning when to hold back and when to step in. It's a kind of dance and I am gradually getting the hang of it.

The basic art class ends in March, along with the first year of the advanced class. The transition is marked by a final feedback session. We are sitting in a local wine bar going through the rating sheets – high praise from all but one of my fifteen students. I immediately feel deflated.

Dave smiles. "Don't take it personally. All your actions generate **results**. Treat it as a learning experience. The question you can ask yourself is, 'What can I do differently next time?'

"Keep in mind that you will never please everyone, no matter what you do. A certain amount of criticism is part of life. Most criticism says more about the person who is complaining than about you. Do the best work possible and trust yourself completely."

"Thanks, Dave. That's worth remembering."

"Regarding your work in the advanced class, it is outstanding. I believe you are practising harder than many of the students. And this reflects a simple and obvious **secret**: the more you practise, the better you get. I think a lot of people are afraid to put in the hours. You seem to be far more focused and motivated than last year."

"Really? That's good to hear." Maybe this VIKAR thing is working after all.

"I would like you to continue tutoring the basic art class. The next one starts in a couple of weeks. Do you think you can handle co-facilitating the intermediate class too?"

"Gosh! Am I ready to handle that level? I don't know. Are you sure? Where would I get the time? That's one extra evening per week."

"Well, just think about it. There's no pressure. And you would be co-facilitating with me. All the new classes start in April, so let me know over the next two weeks."

"It is a very kind and generous offer. I will have to talk to Robert about it. Thank you."

We order another two glasses of the house red and the conversation fades into pleasant small talk. An hour later I am walking home feeling a little bewildered. What is happening? Am I creating this reality?

Disparate thoughts are dashing through my mind. I started these art classes two and a half years ago ... the mystery of a water-goddess who leaves me with more questions than answers ... the uncertainty of Xavier and Loutro ... my relationship with Robert. I really need to talk to someone. Who could possibly understand these confusing emotions and strange experiences?

Lilura. I must give her a call. She is the one person with whom I can share everything. I look at the time; it's not too late.

She picks up in three rings. "Hey, sweetie, is that you?" There is a soft lilt in her voice.

"Yes, aunt, it's me. How are you?"

"All is well this end, dear. How are you?"

I dispense with the formalities. "I need to come up and see you. A lot is going on. I could do with a bit of insight."

"I am free next weekend. Will that suit?"

"Yes, please. I will drive up on Friday. I look forward to it. We can speak then." I ring off, feeling a sense of relief.

Right, one week to go. I will immerse myself in working, painting and reading. Everyday distractions. Lilura is a great listener and will no doubt offer sensible advice.

Robert is away tonight. I light a few candles and play soft relaxing music. A good soaking and a solid night's sleep is just what I need. An hour later I cosy into fresh linen and pull the duvet up over my shoulders.

* * *

Friday arrives at last and I am driving to The Lakes. It is early evening when my car enters the driveway. The sun is already setting and the cottage is bathed in an ethereal light. The first thing I notice is the quietness ... so different from city life. At once a calm comes over me.

Lilura bursts out the front door, runs over and gives me a tight hug. "So good to see you!" she sings, then does a jubilant dance with her arms raised high.

I laugh. "It's good to see you too."

"Come, come, you must be worn out from the drive."

I grab my bag and follow her into the kitchen. The kettle has already boiled. "A cup of tea will set you right. What would you like? Strawberry, peppermint, camomile, lemon and ginger –"

"Peppermint is perfect, thank you."

"How about a piece of freshly made organic carrot cake? It's got that light lemony icing you adore."

"Yes, please."

Soon we are happily conversing over delicious lemon and peppermint aromas. The warm stove creates a relaxing atmosphere. Lilura regales me with tales about her recent ecstatic dance and shamanic journeying workshops. Her face is lit with joy as she describes the various experiences of the participants. I feel a bit envious: here is a woman who truly loves her work.

The inner sigh must have reflected on my face. Another piece of delicious carrot cake slides its way over to me. "More tea, dear?"

"Please."

"Do you want to tell me what's going on?"

I pour the details about Xavier, Loutro, the art classes, the developments with Tethys, and my relationship with Robert. It all gushes out of me for what seems like ages, and I am vaguely aware that Lilura is patiently listening and nodding and making soothing sounds in just the right places.

By the time I am finished I feel a lot better. Talking is wonderfully therapeutic. It's when issues stay pent up, running circles in my mind, that the difficulties arise.

"So what are the biggest issues?"

I pause to look at the kitchen tiles for a few moments. "It's the experience with Xavier; it turned my world upside down. Also I am unsure about this art opportunity. Should I take on more responsibility? Am I good enough? Why does Dave believe in me?"

"Let's go sit in the lounge. Dinner will be ready in an hour."

The fire is bright and welcoming. Dark wooden beams protrude from the ceiling, lending to the quaint character of the cottage. The carmine couch cosily embraces me.

"So tell me about Xavier."

My hands shake with emotion as I spill the details. "I feel so guilty about what happened. I care about Robert. I really do. He's a good man. But Xavier is so different – passionate, alive and affectionate; unfortunately he is also carefree and irresponsible."

"What do you mean by 'irresponsible'?"

"He is a drifter. He seems lost. He is no longer chasing money or prestige but instead is searching for his passion and pleasure."

"A bit like you?" There is a twinkle in her eye.

We stare at the hypnotic flames for a while, then she says, "What have you been chasing for the last two years? When did you last touch fulfilment and pleasure?"

All I can think about is Loutro. My heart and soul feel warm when I remember those days of bliss. Pleasure and fulfilment indeed. But that was a vacation – it's not real life.

"With Robert I have security. He earns well. He is reliable. We are comfortable together. And he has mentioned the possibility of marriage."

"Do you have a lot in common? Do you share any passions?"

"Um ... we enjoy the theatre and ballets and walks ..."

She takes my hand and looks deep into my eyes. "The two most important relationship questions are these: **How does the energy between the two of you feel? Do you share similar passions and values?**"

There is a silent tension. I can feel a tear welling up. I bite my lip and gaze at the fire. Oh my!

And then the dam bursts, and Lilura is holding me while I sob and mutter: "We share similar passions, you know ... art, beaches and oceans ... we both love swimming ... he has a degree in architecture ... it felt so good to be around him ... yes, yes, it is the energy ... that indefinable thing ... I was ignoring it, trying to be sensible ... he seems to know the water-goddess ..."

I suddenly feel really tired. Lilura hands me a box of tissues and pours a couple of single malt whiskeys. A serene energy settles around us and my words falter then disappear into the silence.

A little later we enjoy delectable pieces of organic chicken, peppers, mushrooms, pineapple and tomatoes arranged on brightly coloured skewers, served with new potatoes and a dollop of butter.

The conversation is gentle and easy. After a light dessert we exchange a tender hug and I am off to bed. The last thing I hear is "Sweet dreams" and then I am a gurgling stream swishing through hundreds of gorgeous white lilies.

* * *

I wake up late on Saturday morning, my sprawled body unfurling into a long stretch and yawn. I slide into my dressing gown and stumble downstairs. Aah … the aroma of hot coffee is wafting from the stove.

Lilura is nowhere to be found. There is a note on the table: 'Nipped out to do a few errands. Packed you some snacks in case you venture for a walk.' She is so sweet and thoughtful. I pour some coffee and find the granola. It is nice to have a bit of time to myself.

After breakfast I have a long, steamy shower. My mind is reflecting on last night's revelation. Maybe an amble to the lake will clarify my thoughts. I dry off and find my snuggy jacket, walking boots and journal.

The stroll through the crisp air invigorates me. I sit down on grandfather's wooden bench and look around at the beautiful scenery. Many of the trees are still bare but a few are starting to green. A couple of ducks are floating by on the grey lake.

A babbling sound catches my attention. There is a swirling movement in the water and a familiar figure forms. It is the sensual water-goddess. I smile warmly. "Hello, Tethys."

Hello, Zara. It is good to see you again.

"And you …" I feel like jumping into the water and giving her a squelchy hug.

How is it going with creating your reality?

Can I confide in my water-goddess? Shall I admit my fears and concerns? I look pensively at her, then: "I have been offered to tutor another basic art class and an intermediate class. I don't know if I am good enough. I don't know if I should be devoting so much time to –"

To your dream? To your crystal clear vision?

"Um, yes …"

What is the alternative?

"I focus on my accountancy job, settle down with Robert, paint a little in my spare time, probably get married and have a comfortable life."

It sounds enticing. One of your feet is firmly planted in this reality.

"Yes, it's the world I know. Predictable and pleasant."

Have you forgotten how frustrated, lonely and sad you were two years ago?

"Oh, Tethys! Will this vision happen? Will it be what I want? The dream is vividly painted but how will it be when I get there? I feel scared. I don't know what to expect."

What you are experiencing is a Crisis Of Faith. It's quite natural. Do you remember my words? Every great journey starts with a great root of faith and a great cloud of doubt. Faith and doubt will be your steady companions on your path to fulfilment and peace.

"I am terrified of doing something crazy and irrational, like running away to some island with Xavier."

Your other foot is embedded in the world you desire, in the reality you are creating. It can be confusing when your feet are in different worlds.

"Is this some sort of transition point? What should I do?"

The first thing you need to do is recognise your fear. Then accept your fear as a natural part of the process. Every transition from one reality to another involves an element of faith and an element of fear. Fear is not a reason to walk away from your dream.

I feel a bit desperate. "Please show me what to do."

Open your journal and write this heading: **Keys To Reality Shifting**

1. Self-Belief

Self-belief is the first great key to reality shifting. You have to believe in yourself. You have to believe that you can achieve your dream. If you don't believe in you, who else will?

Self-belief is not the same as self-esteem. Self-esteem is a myth propagated by various segments of society. It is the idea that you should measure and rate yourself against someone else's measuring stick. Magazines, television, films, parents, teachers, religious and cultural entities often extend arbitrary standards and expect you to meet these standards. If you do meet these standards, you receive praise and recognition and 'esteem'; if you don't, you are often made to feel 'less than' or 'worthless'. So please ignore that nonsense. You are far too precious to be judged and measured by another.

Self-belief is simply **faith in yourself**. *It is an attitude that you choose. It is a confident outlook that shines from your inner being. It is an energy that inspires others. It is recognising and allowing the flow of your Heart Song.*

My gaze drifts across the purling water. "That's a lot to take on board but all eminently sensible." These are choices I need to make and keep making: love versus fear, faith versus doubt. I write for a while and feel a stirring of excitement.

Let's do an exercise. Close your eyes and imagine the **Future You**, *a few years down the line. Take as much time as you need while you notice all the details. What are you wearing? Where are you living? What are you doing? Who is around you? What can you hear? How much fulfilment and peace are you feeling?*

It goes quiet for ten minutes as I immerse myself in this visualisation.

Open your eyes. Imagine Future You is sitting opposite you right now. Walk over and step into Future You. Take a deep breath and settle into this wonderful energy. You are Future You. As Future You, write about the journey you made to fulfil your dream. Describe what your life is like now, with whom you are sharing it and what you did to get here. Finally, answer these two questions: Who believed in you? Was the journey worth it?

I am surrounded by calmness and tranquillity while completing this exercise. Afterward I sit with my eyes closed for another fifteen minutes, slowly absorbing the wisdom of the experience.

Then I flick to a special page at the back of my journal entitled **Inspirational Thoughts** and I jot down: 'Yes, I Can!'

Tethys is splashing around in the water. Her movements are quick and steady. I watch her for a few minutes, trying to understand what she is doing. Then I spot a tiny blue butterfly. "You are not trying to catch the butterfly, are you?" She nods carefully.

"It's impossible. You are made of water. That fragile creature seeks a solid landing, a place of stillness." Ignoring my comment, she continues her delicate dance of seduction, trying to find the right way to approach the butterfly. Half an hour goes by. At first I am mildly amused, soon frustrated – patience has never been one of my traits.

I munch an apple ... look at my watch ... tap my foot. Part of me wants to walk into the lake and do the job myself. Finally she holds out her palm and creates a very shallow and tranquil pool of water upon which the butterfly deftly alights and drinks.

What did you learn from watching me?

I feel like a child in school. "Um ... Perseverance? Determination? Don't give up?"

2. Willpower

Who wins in the contest between the rock and the stream?

When you encounter a barrier or an obstacle between you and your dream, you apply willpower. You find a way around the rock. Consider the power of relentlessly flowing water.

Some visions take years to come to fruition. Some dreams take long to achieve. If you are not willing to constantly apply your knowledge, to patiently do what is necessary, to endure, you will slip back into a reality you don't want.

What else did I demonstrate while trying to seduce a butterfly?

The VIKAR presentation drifts into my mind. I close my eyes for a moment to recall the last three words. Oh yes. "Learning! It's more than being persistent and tenacious. When you did not get the result you wanted, you tried something new, you tried something different."

3. Learning

If a strategy is no longer producing the results you desire, try something new. Seek fresh knowledge and apply it. Be open to feedback. Adjust your course. Keep applying, keep observing, keep learning.

Just as faith and doubt will accompany you on your journey, so too will innovation and stagnation. Everything in life is a choice. All your choices create your reality. They create your destiny.

I am scribbling in my journal. It all makes so much sense. I am afraid I have been a bit of a hopeless dreamer at various times of my life – wishing for a miracle to drop out of the sky.

Ah, another inspirational thought: 'I am responsible for my life. If it is going to be, it is up to me!'

You may find it useful to write your inspirational thoughts onto little notes and stick them around your house. This will help you absorb their motivating energy.

I fill my lungs with the fresh air rolling off the lake. My boot swishes playfully in the long grass. There is something quite thrilling and scary about taking responsibility for my life. I no longer need to depend on something mundane or mysterious outside of me. I am the creator of my reality.

I need to leave now. These lessons will integrate and become part of you. Keep in mind that nothing is possible without a great root of faith, a great cloud of doubt, relentless willpower and innovation, and lifelong learning.

I feel such a welling of gratitude in my heart. My hands spontaneously meet on my chest. "I would like to express my deep appreciation for all you have shared. You have opened my mind to wonderful possibilities. I am finally understanding the **secrets** to creating my reality and manifesting my dreams."

Her eyes blink slowly as she solemnly nods. Then she dissolves into the lake and is gone.

I scrawl the last few notes in my journal and meander back to the cottage. Lilura is chopping vegetables in the warm kitchen. I go over and embrace her happily. "Hey, sweetie, did it go well?"

I fill the kettle with water and flip the switch. "Yes, I received most of the answers I need. I feel invigorated and peaceful. Here, let me help you."

"You can grate the Gruyère cheese and crumble the feta, and put it all in this bowl. Oh, and add one raw egg to the mixture."

"Are we making your famous spinach-and-cheese turnovers?"

"Indeed. What kind of tea would you like?"

"Can I try the strawberry?"

A question has been gnawing my mind for so long. I consider how to broach the subject. "How are you coping with mother's passing? Are you still grieving?"

She stuffs the teabags into a large teapot and fills it with boiling water. "Honey, it's been three years. Of course I miss her. Terribly. But I know she has gone to a wonderful place."

"I find it difficult to deal with the loss. I think of her almost every day. I wonder where she is and what she is doing. Death makes life such a mystery."

My aunt thoughtfully stirs the tea. "Peeking beyond the veil is something many of us wish we could do. Grief takes its own time and moves at its own pace. It's different for each one of us. Finally we come to rest in reality-as-it-is. And we get to keep those precious memories."

Here comes the awkward question. "Who is my father?"

"Oh, sweetie," she sighs, looking at me kindly. "Your father was a powerful man who did not want to attract attention to you and your mother. He left when you were very young, believing it was in both of your best interests."

I take a long sip. "Did you ever meet him?"

"Yes, twice. He was an unusual man. Commanding, influential and vulnerable at the same time. He loved your mother with quite a passion."

She drains the pot of spinach using a sieve, then stirs in the mixture of fried onions, garlic, mushrooms and peppers, finally adding the cheese. The finishing touch is a pinch of smoked paprika and salt and pepper.

"Shall I butter the filo sheets?"

"Don't worry, I have it in hand."

I watch her carefully preparing the turnovers. What else can I ask about this mystery man? Why will no one ever talk about him? I want to understand my origins.

As if reading my thoughts, she turns to me and says, "Be patient, sweetie. In time you will discover all you need to know."

The sink fills with hot, soapy water; washing the dishes will be a useful distraction.

"Let me slide these into the oven and then we can relax by the fire."

For the rest of the evening we chat about our favourite books, our dreams and hopes and plans, the boredom of my job, life in the city versus the country, and the relatively new phenomenon of social media.

Dinner is quite delicious. The turnovers are slightly crispy on the outside; moist and juicy on the inside. Baby potatoes and salad are the perfect accompaniment. Dessert is decadent chocolate soufflés served in little glass ramekins.

Lilura does not own a television and seldom goes to a cinema; however, she has an extensive collection of Classical and New Age music. The cottage is usually filled with the sweet orchestral sounds of Bach, Brahms, Debussy or Handel, or the soothing melodies of Terry Oldfield, Peruquois & Praful, Deva Premal & Miten, or other chilled meditation music.

Tonight is no different. Terry Oldfield's 'Yoga Harmony' is cascading blissfully through multiple speakers, hushing us into peaceful quietude. The fire is gently crackling, and for a few moments Xavier's lovely face flashes before me. I wonder what he is doing. I wonder where he is in the world.

* * *

Sundays are the best day of the week. Although I am usually painting or sketching on this day, it is pleasurable to wake up and gaze at the sheep in the field and survey the green hills rolling into the horizon. It is so serene. I don't miss London at all.

Breakfast is an aromatic mix of lightly fried diced onions and potatoes, smoked salmon, and scrambled eggs with a pinch of chives. Fresh air from the open window is breezing through the kitchen.

We are in our dressing gowns, chatting over steaming coffee. I love moments like these. Freely relaxing and connecting with someone special. No posing and preening, no worrying about how we look. It's the way life should be. All I desire is love, romance, friendship, affection and kindness. And being real with significant others. Everything important is right here before us.

Lilura's voice breaks through my reverie. "Did you resolve everything yesterday, sweetie?"

Gosh, Xavier is popping into my head again. "Um, pretty much. I still have no idea what is happening with my love life. I feel torn by feelings of guilt, loyalty, sensibility and desire. I don't know the answers. Not sure if I even know the questions." I giggle at my own silliness.

My aunt looks more solemn. "This is a big issue, honey. Robert is nudging you toward marriage. He has certain expectations and hopes. You need to set your heart straight and make some decisions. It's not all about you."

Ouch. These confusing emotions are pulling me in different directions. Perhaps I am being selfish and self-indulgent.

"When last did you hear from Xavier?"

"Never. I did not give him my details."

"Then how do you know if he is thinking about you? What he may be feeling?"

"Well, he left me a postcard with his details. It may still be in the pouch at the back of my journal."

"Do you think you ought to find it?"

I amble upstairs with a sense of trepidation. I have not looked at the postcard.

Sitting at the kitchen table, I search through the pockets of my journal. Ah, here it is. I gaze at the photo of the beautiful tavernes and pebbled beach. My heart suddenly starts pounding. I turn over the postcard. And here, in his distinctive scrawl, is Xavier's dream. Oh my, it's his Postcard From The Future.

'I am living near the beach in a sunny climate with my soul-mate Zara. We teach art to groups of people who travel to see us. We have two children. I am very happy. My life is complete.'

No! No, no, no, no, no! He couldn't have written that. My face crumples and tears start flowing. It was a holiday romance. He is not the committed type. It can't be true. But my heart knows and tears do not lie.

I am sobbing while Lilura looks kindly at me. She scurries off and returns with a box of lavender tissues. I push the postcard over to her.

"It can't be true. Does he really mean that? I have not seen or heard from him in over nine months!" I feel light-headed and a bit sick.

She puts her hand on mine and smiles. "Cup of tea, dear?"

"Yes ... yes ... anything, peppermint ..."

I am holding my head in my hands, staring at the table. Have I been running away from something? Why have I never contacted him? Will he still be interested in me? Does he feel the same way?

"What am I going to do?"

We sip our tea in the descending silence.

"Can I use your computer?"

"Of course, you know where it is."

I rush over to the study and open my email account. I carefully type in Xavier's address. Gosh, I hope it is still correct. What if he has changed it? I begin to type, then delete, then type, then start all over again. Need to choose my words carefully; first an apology for not contacting him. It takes about forty-five minutes, and finally:

'Dear Xavier

'First of all, sorry for not contacting you. What happened between us left me blissfully happy and utterly confused. You opened the door and showed me a glimpse of my dream life. Then all my fears and issues surfaced. I guess I wasn't ready to face everything. I am embarrassed to admit that I only read your postcard this morning.

'Perhaps you feel I cut you off, perhaps you are angry. I don't know. You have probably moved on to another relationship. I have no idea what to say, except that I am sorry, it was not you, it was me.

'I hope you are happy. Hope you are finding your passion and pleasure.

'Fondest memories
Zara x'

I hover over the send button for ages and then take a deep breath and click. Oh my, it's gone. No stopping it now. What will he think? Should I be opening this door again? Will he ever respond?

I locate my aunt and embrace her warmly. "Thank you. For everything."

We spend the morning looking through old photo albums, then take a short walk across the fields. There is not much to say about my romantic life. It's my issue and my decision and I need to resolve it.

After a delectable home-made tomato soup with spelt-and-rye bread, I pack my bag and load the car. It's an effusive goodbye with a lingering hug. I am finding it harder to leave this time. Has my bond with Lilura strengthened? Or is it a deepening affinity with The Lakes?

It's a long drive back with plenty of time to mull over the various aspects of my life and the remarkable teachings of Tethys. There is a way past this transition point and my Crisis Of Faith. I will move forward and manifest my Heart Song.

* * *

I am back in London and run off my feet. Year Two of the advanced art class commenced in April. On top of this, one evening per week is devoted to tutoring a basic art class and one evening to co-tutoring the intermediate art class. Accountancy fills my days and art fills my evenings and weekends.

Robert never complains, which still surprises me. I have come to understand that we are good companions but we will never be passionate and we don't share the same dreams. He is not initiating any further marriage discussion so I am pleased and rather relieved. I have heard nothing from Xavier; perhaps I have just been foolish.

It is the month of May. Warmer weather has started arriving in England so I am storing our jackets and unpacking the summer clothes from the loft. I adore these seasonal transitions. It is Friday evening and Robert is away until Tuesday; once the clothes are sorted I nip onto the internet to surf for news and entertainment.

I hear the familiar ping of an email arriving so I click to the inbox. My heart stops. It's Xavier! The email preview simply says 'Hello'. I am afraid to open it. What took him so long to respond? Will the message be unpleasant or patronising? Is he going to let me down gently?

I go to the kitchen and brew a cup of black tea. I add a dollop of honey and a dash of whiskey to steady my nerves. Should I talk to Lilura first? No, I can't bother her with my nonsense. I have a sudden craving for chocolate. Gosh, what is wrong with me?

I walk over to my computer, sit down, then get up again for a box of tissues. Finally I am ready. Please, please, let it not be bad news. I reach over and tentatively click open the email:

'Hello Zara, it is so good to hear from you! I was worried that I had hurt or insulted you in some way. It was some relief to receive your email.

'I have been sailing a yacht down to Florida and have not been checking my old email account, hence this delayed response.

'I feel we shared something magnificent in the short time we had together. You are still the one I think about every day.

'Yours, Xavier xx'

I am staring at the message with astonishment. I cannot believe that he thinks about me every day, that he still has feelings for me. My world is turning upside down again. I read the email over and over, devouring every drop, every nuance, every hidden meaning. Then I make another cup of tea and sit in my wingback chair for a long time.

Eventually I hit the reply button and write:

'Hello Xavier

'Receiving your email was a lovely surprise. I was unsure what you felt about our time in Loutro.

'I am very busy with the advanced art class and am now tutoring the basic and intermediate levels. In some ways, art seems to have become my life. It brings me much happiness and peace.

'I feel I should be honest with you. I am still living with Robert. He is a good man and I do not want to hurt him.

'I know your lifestyle is a bit unusual but I would love to stay in contact.

'Warm regards
Zara xx'

I read the email again after I send it. Is it too formal? Too cool? I have no idea what I am doing and my emotions are all over the place. Perhaps the best solution is a good soaking. I turn on the taps and sprinkle my favourite bath salts into the steaming water, then light a few scented candles and search for a glossy magazine.

I am laying here thinking about Xavier. Is it wrong to follow my heart? Should I cease all communication out of respect for Robert? Is it cheating to stay connected by email? Then I realise that I might lose all contact with Xavier if I cut him off again. I can't bear the thought. A foot in each reality ... oh my, I am going to have to manage it somehow.

An hour later I am deeply relaxed and tipsy from a smooth, smoky whiskey. I step out of the bath, pat myself dry and lay naked on the bed. There is that familiar ping again. I open the email:

'Hello Zara. I completely respect your situation and will leave our communication in your hands. If you no longer wish to email, please let me know. I will understand.

'It is fabulous to read about your progress in the art classes. Congratulations! I have seen how you paint when you let go and let your passion run free. Keep trusting your heart – it will serve you well.

'Love, Xavier xx'

I read his message a few times. Perhaps it's the relaxing bath, or perhaps the whiskey, that is causing tingles to gently ripple through my body. I close my eyes and listen to the soft whispers of the Mediterranean sea ... feel the warm sun drenching my thighs ... hear the sound of my lover's voice ... breathe in his scent ... sense his hands caressing me ... surrender to the sweet and sexy dance of his fingers. My stomach tightens as the luscious tingles overwhelm me ... I bite my lower lip ... oh ... my ...

* * *

There is a lovely surprise when I arrive for Monday's art class. Michaela is visiting for a few days and will be co-tutoring the advanced group. She is a warm and friendly person and I find her art critique insightful and useful.

After the class she invites me for a drink. Dave needs to work late and Robert is still away so I eagerly accept the opportunity to socialise. We stroll to the nearby wine bar and Michaela orders an expensive Château Les Ormes de Pez, which turns out to be a generous and fruity evening companion.

It is marvellous to discuss art with someone so experienced and I am asking plenty of questions. I wonder how she started her art school in Europe. Is it difficult to open a school? Is it expensive to run? How does she attract students? She kindly advises me for the next hour and finishes with some encouragement: "You have the right combination of talent and people-skills to run your own classes. The rest is simply a matter of doing thorough research and then taking a leap of faith."

We finish the Claret and the conversation eases into a few giggly moments. Soon we are fondly remembering the gorgeous holiday in Loutro. "Whatever happened to Xavier?" she asks. "It seemed you two got on very well." I blush slightly at the awkwardness of the situation. "It's difficult, Michaela. I am still living with Robert here in London and he is keen to progress our relationship."

Another bottle of red arrives with fresh glasses. I gaze across the room at a couple intimately chatting in a shady corner. I sigh deeply. "Something special happened in Loutro. It left me feeling confused and guilty for months. Last Friday, Xavier and I swapped emails for the first time … and it felt really good."

She leans forward and there is kindness in her voice. "These situations can be very difficult. I guess you can't talk to many people about it. I had a similar predicament a while ago and it took more than a year to resolve."

"Really? What did you do?"

"I discovered this truth: I am a unique puzzle piece and need to **find the person who best fits with me**. There are plenty of people who are fine companions but they are better kept as friends. I chose the person who felt like the best match, the one who made my heart sing."

"Are you saying you have a lot in common?"

"Definitely. We both love art, hiking and skiing. I think it helps if you share similar passions. It means you actually enjoy having a conversation, instead of tolerating a topic that is completely uninteresting. We also share liberal views and are mildly spiritual."

"Similar passions and values ..."

"Indeed. And most important to me, he is tactile and affectionate. I thrive on regular touch, hugs and kissing. I have come to understand the importance of kissing in a romantic relationship. I mean *passionate kissing*, not the rushed good morning or goodbye peck strewn among the busyness of everyday life."

The wine is making me feel warm and dreamy and my thoughts drift to a dusky beach. "With the right partner, kissing is very sensual, intimate and connecting."

"Exactly! Let me share a little **secret** with you. Every week we arrange a sacred Love Session, a time when we will be undisturbed for a couple of hours. This is an appointment that is planned, agreed and diarised ahead of time, and we both take great care to attend. During the session we light candles or incense and play our favourite relaxation music. There is no agenda. We use the time for sensual massage, gentle all-over body stroking, making love ... whatever flows. It's so nurturing and fulfilling."

"What a wonderful idea! If we don't make time in our busy lives for sensual connection, it just slips away." I must talk to Robert about this.

"Have you ever played the 'Yes, Please – No, Thank You' game? It is one of my favourite pleasures."

I shake my head. "Tell me ..."

"Arrange a Love Session that is at least two hours long. Set up the bedroom with flowers and candles and gentle music. Make sure the temperature is warm and comfortable because both of you will be naked the entire time. Allot an equal time period, perhaps forty-five minutes each. During your time period your partner lavishes on you whatever he thinks you might enjoy. Your job is only to receive, not to do anything. You will give regular feedback to your partner using only four phrases: 'Yes, please' (I am really loving what you are doing); 'Yes' (I like what you are doing); 'Maybe' (I am unsure if I like what you are doing); 'No, thank you' (I do not like what you are doing; stop it)."

"Won't my partner feel annoyed or upset by hearing a 'No, thank you'?"

"The **secret** is to not take any feedback personally. The person receiving is merely saying 'At this moment, I am enjoying this or not enjoying this'. Our pleasure needs can change from minute to minute, and this exercise allows both partners to stay in the moment. Of course you must remember to swap around when your time period is up."

"So the receiving partner does nothing but lay there and get pampered?"

"Yes. It is a brilliant experience on so many levels. Many of us have no idea how to express our needs or how to simply receive pleasure. This helps us to do both."

I giggle to myself. I am discussing sex and pleasure in an English wine bar. I must be a bit inebriated.

"One last **secret** I have learned: Slow down all movement. The intense stimulation of everyday life means that we often lose the ability to exquisitely sense what is happening. Our bodies want to really notice and savour every sensual stroke, every tantalising touch and every gorgeous caress. Slowing down conserves the energy of the giver and helps the receiver profoundly tune into each pleasurable sensation."

"That sounds so liberating." I sigh. Sex is such a natural and beautiful part of love. There must be plenty we can learn about fulfilling our needs and increasing our pleasure.

Michaela is great fun and we chat until Dave finally joins us. We order a last drink and the conversation slips back into painting, tutoring and the upcoming art vacation in November. Details are being finalised and should be on the board next week. I wonder where in the world it will be.

A bell rings to signal closing time. We exchange hugs and smiles and Dave and Michaela disappear into the night. As for me, I amble home, feeling like I haven't a care in the world.

* * *

The next five months settle into a comfortable routine. I am practising self-belief and persevering through the time and relationship pressures resulting from my demanding art schedule. I am feeling more confident in my ability to coach and mentor the students, and the feedback is heartening.

Dave kindly organises a gallery showing of the advanced students' work and I manage to sell two of my paintings for a decent price. It's enough to pay for the impending art vacation.

Robert's business is flourishing and he is away a great deal. I think this is helping me cope with the stress of maintaining two romantic relationships. There has been a flurry of emails. Xavier is as vague as ever about his activities, which range from sailing yachts to assisting at a diving school. I wonder if he will ever settle down.

I am sitting on my bed at the end of a long week. The flyer for the art vacation lies blazing before me: 'The islands of the Bahamas form a 100,000-square-mile archipelago that extends over 500 miles of the clearest water in the world. It consists of 700 islands, including the three islands known as North, South and East Bimini. The name Bimini means Mother Of Many Waters in the Taino Native American Indian language of the Caribbean.'

The familiar ping of an email interrupts my reading. I open the message:

'Hello Zara. Yes, I will be attending the North Bimini vacation in November. I imagine you are apprehensive about seeing me again; don't worry, I am too. Let's have no expectations and no agenda and we'll see how things go. I am very much looking forward to seeing you again. Much love, Xavier xxx.'

My tummy does a flip flop. I want to see him again but I am filled with trepidation. What if he no longer likes me? What if I don't feel the same way? What if our connection is stronger than before? Where will it lead?

The last couple of weeks melt away and suddenly I am organising a taxi and doing last-minute packing. Robert hugs me fiercely as we say goodbye. I step into the waiting car and hear the door quietly close. My mind is flooded with anxious thoughts. This relationship confusion has gone on too long. I am determined to make some hard choices before the end of the year. Tears begin streaming down my face. The driver tactfully ignores me.

* * *

It's a long flight from London to Fort Lauderdale International Airport in Florida, USA, then a brief overnight stay and a short flight to the island the next morning. We are a larger group this time, ten English delegates plus Dave, and the mood is buoyant.

Flying over Bimini is spectacular. I survey the wonderful scenery: glistening white beaches, azure waters that flow into greens and turquoises, and swaying coconut palms. A boat transfers us to North Bimini. The ocean breeze is fluttering my hair while the warm sun lavishes its luxurious rays upon my skin. I am filled with excitement and apprehension.

We drop our bags in the large house and join Michaela with her eleven European students in the dining area. It is good to see her again and I bounce over and give her a big hug. There are jubilant greetings and introductions and then Dave cracks open the champagne and fills twenty-three glasses with bubbly and orange juice. One glass remains empty on the table.

"To a fabulous art vacation. May you produce great masterpieces!"

There is a raising of glasses and cheering. For the next half-hour everyone is chatting away with a mix of exuberance and anticipation. Then Dave taps a glass and we quieten down. He explains that we should use today to settle in, unpack and explore the island. We will meet here in the dining room tomorrow for breakfast at nine and start painting at ten. This will be the daily routine, with a packed lunch at one, and the rest of the day dependent on our location.

After a bit more socialising most of us amble off to unpack. We are spread out over adjacent houses. The rooms are shared between two people and I have yet to meet my room-mate. The magnificent beach and aquamarine sea are beckoning me through the open window. I long to go for a walk but have been invited to join a driving tour of the island.

I grab my sunglasses and bag and meet the others outside. Before me idles a salmon-pink open-top jeep emblazoned with colourful fish and we all have a laugh while climbing aboard. John appoints himself navigator and location announcer and begins to regale us with facts about the islands.

Our new homes are located near the top of North Bimini and we are driving south along a narrow strip. Marinas for pleasure yachts and small boats are predominantly on the east side, in the protected bay hugged by both arms of the island. Most of the gorgeous beaches appear to be on the west side.

We soon reach Bailey Town, the main residential area complete with a variety of stores. A little further on is Alice Town, which is the centre of the tourist trade, displaying several marinas, hotels, bars and restaurants. The drive down Queen's Highway takes us to the southern tip of the island and we stop to gaze at South Bimini across the water. That island is quieter and is home to a small airport, yacht club and resort.

We cruise back into Alice Town to explore the shops and walk along the shore. The students are great fun and the afternoon drifts into wild splashing in the warm sea and cool conversations on the beach. We spend time admiring stunning yachts in the marinas and around five o'clock settle for cocktails at a waterside restaurant. The sun is already setting so we decide to stay for a delicious seafood dinner.

I am wondering what happened to Xavier.

* * *

It is morning and the jovial atmosphere has continued through to breakfast. It turns out that the main house provides a buffet in the mornings, a set menu in the evenings, as well as a packed lunch for our daily excursions. If we choose not to attend a meal we should let the hosts know. We are free to eat out on Saturday night.

After breakfast Dave and Michaela depart in their own vehicle, which carries all the easels, pallets, paints and other equipment. The rest of us squeeze into the pink jeep and a couple of golf carts, while some of the fitter students opt for hired bicycles. Then we all trundle down the road to the Bimini Bay Marina. The subject for today is 'sailing'.

When we arrive, everyone breaks into pairs or small groups to find the most appealing boat to paint or sketch. I am not in the mood for company so I walk to the furthest point of the harbour. It is lovely breathing the fresh sea air and feeling the sun on my bare arms.

I am staring at a shimmering sleek yacht with two huge white sails and dark tinted windows. 'Spirit of Atlantis' is written in curvy blue letters along the side. There are no boats behind it and the backdrop is open turquoise sea. Perfect. I set up my easel and chair and open my painting bag.

"It's a beautiful boat, isn't it?" I hear the soft, smooth voice to my right. "Indeed," I reply. My heart is suddenly racing and a tingle rushes into my tummy. I look up and drop the pallet, then stare for a moment, unable to move.

"Hello, you." He stretches out his arms. "Come here."

"Xavier ..." I move toward him and we share a long embrace. "How I've missed you."

"It's wonderful to see you again." His voice is gentle and heartfelt. "I have my sketchpad. Do you mind if I join you?"

"Be my guest." And then we are seated, creating side by side, like the sixteen months apart never existed. I remember his energy now, his presence, and how it makes me feel. So peaceful and content.

After a couple of hours of idle conversation and bland brushwork, I realise that I am not focusing on my painting. In fact it's the last thing on my mind. The day is getting warmer and my body is thirsting. Oh! In my haste to escape the others I forgot my packed lunch and water.

"What's up, sweetheart?" He is gently staring at me, obviously a little amused.

"I forgot my water, that's all."

"Come with me ..." He smiles, grabs my hand and walks me aboard the yacht.

"Are you sure you're allowed to do this?" I ask hesitantly.

"Silly, this is my home."

"Seriously?"

"Of course. Welcome to the galley and my stainless steel fridge-freezer. What would you like? Beer, a cold drink, sparkling water, plain water?"

"Sparkling, please. Is this really yours? Do you own it?"

"Yep, it's all mine. A top-of-the-range Leopard 44 catamaran, all 12.98 metres of her. Would you like a tour?"

The yacht is fabulous. Soft recessed lighting; rich cherry wood finishes; surprisingly spacious interior; open-plan kitchen ('galley' in boat-speak) with all the modcons; lounge ('saloon' in boat-speak) with settee that seats eight guests around a dining table; and large windows which provide panoramic views and abundant natural light.

Downstairs are two guest bedrooms ('cabins' in boat-speak), each sleeping two people ('double-berth' in boat-speak), replete with own toilet ('head' in boat-speak), washbasin and shower. The luxurious owner's suite, also downstairs, features a spacious master bedroom, lounge area with couch, study area, plenty of storage and the en suite washroom.

"Do you have to say everything in boat-speak?" I am giggling now. We go back upstairs and sit on the deck at the front of the boat. It is such a flat boat and feels so stable. Xavier cracks open a beer and I sip my sparkling water.

"The thing about a catamaran is that it has two hulls – those boat bottoms on each side – which make the boat rock less. It is unusual for anyone to feel seasick on board. And the way the back of the boat lowers to the water lends itself to easy scuba-diving or snorkelling access; you can just crawl out of the water onto the yacht."

"It is stunning. I had no idea you lived on a boat."

We sit for a long while in the 'forward cockpit lounging area' under the 'fixed overhead hardtop cover' and gaze across the light blue sea. It is a beautiful day and we both need to talk and reconnect. A couple of beers and a few sandwiches later, we are laughing like old friends.

Eventually we return to our painting and sketching but our hearts are not in it. So we stow our art gear in the boat and join the others. Xavier introduces himself to those he does not know and the afternoon is a pleasant mix of playful jesting and bonding with the rest of the group.

At four o'clock we pack up everything and make our way to the main house. Everyone disappears to enjoy some personal time until cocktail hour at six. I invite Xavier to shower in my room and we chat for a while afterward.

Dinner with twenty-four people is quite an affair. Wine and beer lubricate the raucous discussions around the two long tables. The chef has prepared lobster curry followed by banana pudding, a simple but very satisfying meal.

Later in the evening Xavier borrows a bike and cycles back to his boat. Part of me wishes he had asked to stay the night. I retire to my room feeling a curious mix of deep longing and intense happiness. It is not long before the swooshing waves lure me into a world of swirling indigo dreams.

* * *

Today it's back to the marina so it all works out rather well. The moment we arrive, I collect two packed lunches and bottled water and head over to the beautiful catamaran.

I board the yacht and Xavier greets me from ... oh yes, from the galley, where fresh coffee is brewing. He gives me a big kiss. "Good morning, gorgeous. How are you feeling today?"

"Wonderfully rested." I hide a yawn behind my hand, then raise my arms in a big stretch. "Sleep comes easy near the ocean."

He hands me a cup of steaming coffee and we move to the outside lounging area. Soft waves are gently curling around the boat and the sound is quite delicious. I gaze out over the expansive turquoise sea. My heart is purring.

"Your yacht is absolutely fabulous. What a lifestyle it must allow."

"Yes ... I spend a fair amount of time sailing yachts across the world to new owners; sometimes I am returning a yacht home to Florida or some other coastal city. When I am not sailing, I work at the diving school in South Bimini as an instructor. A boat is a fitting home for me. I can live where I want."

"Do you ever think of settling down?"

"I am settling down, right here in Bimini. I love the warm climate ... the beaches ... the wide open space. Do you know that North Bimini is only seven miles long? I am surrounded by the ocean."

I am intrigued. "What does it take to live here? A particular citizenship?"

Xavier laughs. "You're full of questions. The Bahamas is an independent country, part of the British Commonwealth. You are a citizen of the United Kingdom so for shorter stays of a few months you don't need a tourist or business visa. If you wish to apply for permanent residency, you need to purchase property under the International Persons Landholding Act. Oh yes, there is one other benefit of living in the Bahamas: no income tax, capital gains tax or inheritance tax."

"Really?" I am quite surprised.

"Are we going to paint or what?" he says teasingly.

"Yes, of course."

We set up the easel a short distance from the boat. As is often the case, I will be painting while he sketches. We unpack the paint, charcoal and chalk, and soon the creativity starts flowing. I take in the magical surroundings: perfect blue sky, slatted wooden jetty, emerald waters, white yacht. How will I manage to capture all this beauty?

We have different styles and it is useful peeking at each other's work from time to time and trading inspiring comments. A lovely stillness seems to fill the air as we immerse ourselves in brushstroke and drawing. Our lunch break is spent chatting amiably on the boat.

At the end of the day we spend a little time critiquing our work, then pack our equipment and take it down to Dave's van. I borrow a bicycle so that we can cycle back to the house together.

Xavier caresses my neck tenderly. "Why don't we cycle around for a while? We have plenty of time. The sun will not set for another hour."

I nod thoughtfully. "That's a lovely idea."

We hop on the bikes and head south to Porgy Bay, on the eastern side of the island. When we arrive he smiles happily. "I adore this beach."

We kick off our sandals, strip to our swimwear and walk to the water's edge. He takes my hand and leads me knee-deep into the cool sea. And then he kisses me. Fully, passionately, exquisitely. I feel his strong hands on my back and the softness of his lips melting into mine.

"I've missed you, Zara." His eyes are warm and gentle.

"Come with me." He swims out about a hundred yards and I follow. There is still plenty of light in the sky and the sandy ocean floor is easily visible. He hesitates, then dives down deep, and soon we are enveloped in the clear tranquil water.

It's the high-pitched squeal I notice first. Xavier is hovering three yards underwater, an expectant look on his face. There is a dark cloud forming in the distance. Soon a troupe of frivolous dolphins are cascading around us, all cute smiles and eyes that see right through to the soul.

They playfully surf the waves and pirouette beneath the surface; a spontaneous ballet of ocean dancers, replete with an opus of clicks and whistles. It takes me a while to realise that I am crying with joy and experiencing a vague but wondrous sense of coming home. Eventually they disappear into the darkening sea.

We swim to shore and repose on the warm sand. He asks no questions and I cannot find words to share my feelings. We gaze reflectively at the softening horizon, then take a slow ride home, shower and join the others for dinner. The atmosphere is more relaxed tonight; it seems the silken blanket of the Bahamas has enfolded us all.

After dinner Xavier and I chat for some time, then he hops on his bike and I find myself alone again. I stare at the ceiling as the events of the day blaze radiantly through my mind. There is a divine feeling in my spirit. For a moment I think of reading my book; instead I succumb to a soft pillow and the seduction of the soporific sea.

* * *

I wake up feeling fantastic. Breakfast is already underway, so I find some granola and sit outside to watch the new sun sparkling across the sea. There are a few light clouds in the sky and it is lovely and warm. The memory of the dolphin troupe is still dancing sweetly in my mind.

After breakfast everyone deposits their bags in Dave's van. I wedge myself alongside the easels and pallets and settle down for the short ride. Today we are working on a beach on the western side of Bailey Town and when we erupt from our vehicles we are greeted by a spectacular vista.

I am awestruck by the breathtaking scenery ... silver ripples stretching out lazily on miles of azure sea ... soft white sand scrunching delicately underfoot ... friendly palms reaching out for a quiet conversation ... a gentle breeze whispering through pink bougainvilleas ... all portraying a blissful paradise.

Xavier arrives on his bicycle and we separate from the group, walking to the far end of the beach. There is a quiet, secluded spot and it is not long before we are wearing nothing but our sarongs ... and gently kissing and painting. There is something about balmy weather that makes the body feel dreamy and sensual.

I reach out and brush a red streak of paint along his back. It looks beautiful, rippling its way past his muscular shoulders and down his spine. A few moments later he strokes a splash of blue across my tummy and the tingling sensation runs down my thighs. Our eyes meet and spark an unspoken message.

He pushes me against the palm tree and presses his warm body to mine ... his fingers begin tracing a delicate path along my face. Time stands still as we drift into a world of slow, wet, luscious kisses. Hungry lips journey along my neck and down my shoulders. He falls to his knees and I feel his tongue softly caressing my belly ... then his hands grip my bottom and he begins to paint a juicy canvas using delicious, flat brushstrokes.

My legs are trembling as I glance around to make sure we are alone. His curled hair is peeping through my fingers. I bite my lower lip and gasp quietly. My thighs tighten and a warm energy spreads along my back. I want to scream his name but all I hear is that familiar swoosh silhouetted against the sky.

After a moment of delicate lingering, he stands up and kisses me with such passion that it feels like my heart could burst. His hands feather onto my shoulders and he pauses to gaze into my soul. The words "I love you" trickle into my consciousness as we melt into a dizzying embrace.

The rest of the day is relaxing and easy. Our art work flows in a Zen-like manner, the brushstrokes landing with precision and grace and the colours blending as if the presence of the painters was totally unnecessary.

We have plenty of water, fruit and sandwiches and when the bell rings at four o'clock to gather the students, the last thing we feel like doing is leaving. We trudge reluctantly to join the group and I climb aboard the pink jeep. Xavier cycles back to the house.

After a sultry shower, we are laying on the bed together. "I never did find out who my room-mate is ... What are you grinning about?" He reaches over and ruffles my wet hair. "It's me, silly! I paid the other half of your room in case things worked out with us."

I smile at him. "That's sweet. Thank you."

My face is near his bare chest. I move closer and start planting soft kisses. My body feels alive and tingly and wants to finish what we started on the beach. I straddle him and lean forward to kiss his beautiful mouth. The towel unwraps and his hands gently embrace my hips. We close our eyes and immerse ourselves in the deepening pleasure; soon I am a wave flowing gently on the sea of love.

Afterward we cuddle in each other's arms for ages, then dress and enjoy another delectable Caribbean dinner with our deeply relaxed classmates. Over a scrumptious rum-soaked cake Xavier suggests that we spend the night together. I ask if we can sleep on his yacht and he smiles agreeably.

The night is bathed in the nurturing fire of love and the soft lulling of the ocean. We fall asleep happily curled in each other's arms.

* * *

There is no art class today so we awaken slowly over a leisurely breakfast on the boat's front deck. Steaming coffee, scrambled eggs, buttery toast and fresh ocean air. It's a wonderful way to start the morning.

Xavier reaches over and kisses me. "Would you like to go to Porgy Bay again? I can pack us a picnic. How about seafood salad and champagne?"

"That sounds lovely. I am a little tired of sandwiches."

Soon we are cruising on our bicycles through the friendly Caribbean village. The small beach is intimate and welcoming. We amble along until we find a comfortable spot, then lay out a large picnic blanket and pin down the corners.

I reach for his hand. "Let's stroll along the shore for a while. Perhaps we will see the dolphins again."

The rippling wavelets are gently caressing our ankles as we gaze over the aquamarine sea. A warm sun is beaming upon us and my heart feels full and happy. "I never want this to end," I sigh.

"It doesn't have to end. We can plan a life together."

There is a sudden swishing and swirling as a sensual woman forms just ahead of us. "Hello, Tethys!" I call out.

Greetings. I came to see how your lives are progressing.

Xavier is quiet but not startled; he has met the water-goddess before. It is me who speaks. "Things are good. I have come a long way. Almost finished the advanced art classes – only a few months left. Feeling clearer about my vision and dreams."

Write this heading in your journal when you have the opportunity:
Harmonising My Life

In recent years, you have embraced a mix of emotion, exploration and indecision, and you have been pulled in many different directions. It's time to make decisions.

You will recall my words: You are here to THRIVE, not merely survive. You are here to LIVE. Every moment of every day you choose the life you are living. Your future is the result of the choices you make now.

"For the first time in my adult life, I feel like I am touching happiness. I am closer to what I desire. Love, art, teaching, the ocean ..."

Most stress, anxiety and depression is caused by being in the wrong profession and in the wrong relationship. When you discover then heed the call of your Heart Song, you will move toward deeper fulfilment and joy.

This is one of the greatest Heart Song **secrets**: *You need to do work that you love and be with the right romantic partner. Also, it is helpful to surround yourself with people who are like you.*

"That is such beautiful wisdom. Why haven't I realised this before?"

To harmonise your life, start thinking about your **needs**. *What work would fill you with peace and joy? What is it you wish to experience in life? Do you enjoy being nurtured? Do you want a partner who understands your need for affection and physical caressing, without a sexual agenda? Do you want deep love and passion? Do you have at least one or two friends with whom you can share your deepest fears and dreams? Do you know someone who truly listens to you, without pushing advice or solutions onto you? Do you have friends with similar interests and values?*

She turns to Xavier. *What is it you wrote on your postcard?*

He responds calmly. "I am living near the beach in a sunny climate with my soul-mate Zara. We teach art to groups of people who travel to see us. We have two children. I am very happy. My life is complete."

Do you still feel that way?

"I do."

Life is about **prioritising**. *There are many choices that flood your awareness. However, true opportunities come across your path infrequently. Notice when something or someone connects deeply with your soul. Choose carefully and follow your heart. The wise person seizes those opportunities.*

"What do you mean?" I ask.

You need to be clear about what you want in life, and what you are prepared to live without.

"Why can't we have it all?"

If you choose wisely, you will enjoy that which is fulfilling and long-lasting. The question you need to be asking yourself is: **What really matters to me?**

As that thought is lingering in my mind, Tethys fades into the water and disappears. Xavier and I are left with lots of questions and much to talk about. We go for a long swim, then return to the picnic blanket and feast on seafood salad and sparkling water.

He pulls the pad and pencils from the backpack. "Let's sketch out some ideas. Tell me about your needs."

"Um … write down 'art tutoring' … 'family' … 'friends' … 'romance' … 'love' … 'passion' … and 'the ocean'. Now what about you?"

He is drawing the words in bubbles across the large sheet. "Hmm, I like those … I am going to add 'diving' … 'snorkelling' … 'dive tutoring' … 'sunny climate' … and 'dolphins' … and I will add 'Bimini' … I love it here."

We look at the paper together. Suddenly I can see my life forming. At once I feel thrilled and frightened. I turn to look at Xavier. "Do you truly wish to share your life with me?"

He takes my hand. "I do. You are the one for me. I knew this within days of meeting you in Loutro. We have many similar interests and values. And most important of all … you make my heart sing."

We hold each other closely; a delightful energy is moving between us.

In a whispered tone, I wonder: "Does this mean I have to give up my great job and solid income? And leave the city that has been my home for so long? And the –" I catch myself. I remember Tethys' teaching about the price tag and her sage words: *You need to be clear about what you want in life, and what you are prepared to live without.*

"I am scared, Xavier. Moving into my dream means losing other things. And I don't know if it will all work out."

"Everything we do involves faith and doubt, love and fear. They are part of life. Always will be."

I need to be brave. I look at the sheet again. "What are we creating here?"

Xavier begins. "I think we both want to live in Bimini, yes?" I nod. "It has the climate we love, the beaches, the beautiful ocean …" I nod again.

"My boat is paid up. The only expenses are insurance, tax and maintenance. I moor for free because of the diving work. We just need food and love." He winks at me and smiles. "How do you feel about living on a boat?"

"I would never have imagined it, but I love the idea."

"So are we agreeing that we wish to live together on my yacht in Bimini?"

Wow, is this really happening to me? Is this what transpires when a dream arrives? It's decision time. "Yes ... I choose to share my life with you in Bimini." My heart is racing and my tummy is flip-flopping.

He looks at the large sheet. "All that remains is to work out how we will make a living."

I rub my chin thoughtfully. "Hmm ... the Bahamas has lovely weather almost all year round. It's a brilliant holiday destination. What about offering art vacations? Week-long opportunities to improve basic and intermediate skills."

"Great idea. And why not offer diving holidays too? And swimming with dolphins? My catamaran is large enough to support group excursions. I am qualified and experienced. We are both very good swimmers."

"Yes, yes! We will need a website. It's an essential part of business these days. And I am an accountant so I can handle the books and finances. Do you know anyone who can build a website?"

"A guy here in Bimini built and maintains my yacht-delivery website. It even has online payment facilities, direct into my bank account. He could create a new one for us. We just need lots of beautiful photographs of the ocean, dolphins, easels, pallets ... and you and me."

"That leaves the accommodation issue. We can partner with hotels and houses on the island, like the place we are staying at now."

"Yes, and we will partner with the diving school too. Our main income will be from the tutoring."

"Gosh, this could work. We will need to draw up a schedule of vacation slots. Very little capital outlay is required … just advertising."

I write a To Do list: photos, website, seek partners, vacation schedule, advertising. I suddenly think of Lilura – she has experience in these matters. I shall have to call her when I get back to London.

We look at the list together and agree to collect the photos, talk to potential partners and build a rough website before the vacation is over. I have this happy and slightly sick feeling in my tummy. Faith and doubt, love and fear. I smile to myself. I can do this.

I reach into the picnic hamper for the champagne and glasses. "This seems rather appropriate now. Will you open it?"

The cork pops and I rescue it to keep as a memento. He pours the bubbly and proclaims a toast: "To hope, faith and love … but the greatest of these will be our love." We clink the glasses, quaff jubilantly and refill them.

Then I place my glass in the sand and jump on him, smothering him with loving, playful kisses. "I feel so different when I am with you. So different to London and that other life." A small tear is forming in the corner of my eye. "I love you … with all my heart."

I lay my head on his chest while he ruffles my hair. We gaze at the gorgeous sky and listen to the purling waves. The sun gently soothes and relaxes my apprehension … until finally a luscious siesta settles upon us.

When we awaken it is already sunset, so we pack our stuff in the fast-receding light and cycle back to the house. I feel lost in thought ... I am about to move into a whole other world. It's weird and crazy and wonderful.

The evening follows the same routine of shower, socialising and dinner. I am not fully present; I guess part of me is still trying to adapt to this shifting reality. Later we retire to the yacht. Tonight I am realising that this will be my new home and I will be sharing it with the man I love.

* * *

It's Saturday morning and over breakfast Dave and Michaela announce a 'freestyle weekend'. We can go wherever we like and paint whatever we choose, and the tutors will assess the entire week's work on Monday afternoon. Oh my, I better examine and touch up my paintings. We are also told to meet at seven o'clock tonight at a restaurant in Alice Town for dinner.

The weekend turns into an extraordinarily fun bustle of wild photos, conversations with the diving school and accommodation hosts, sketches of our website, a fabulous group meal accompanied by raucous merriment, and a gorgeous shared painting of the two of us at Porgy Bay.

On Monday morning we hastily critique each other's work and make the necessary corrections and improvements. By the afternoon we are tentatively waiting for the tutors. There is a lengthy inspection, and apart from the usual constructive feedback, I am relieved that both Xavier and I receive lavish praise and encouragement.

It is still early afternoon when our tutors finish, so we cycle over to the website designer, download the photos and knock together a rough website. I want lots of colour but Xavier prefers serene blues, so we agree on a background theme of the beach and sea for the entire website and splashes of colour for the art vacations page. The painting of us at Porgy Bay will feature prominently.

We nip back to the house for showers and dinner and then spend the evening on the yacht. Xavier produces a mature Rioja, which is gentle and elegant with smoky leathery flavours, and we spend a couple of hours talking and giggling and kissing. I have no idea how the future will unfold, but right now I feel very happy.

* * *

Tuesday is quite stormy. I am not used to weather like this in Bimini. Dave announces that he and Michaela will act as semi-nude models for today's session, much to the amusement of everyone. The class is divided into two, and Xavier and I move with Michaela to another house.

Our tutor has no qualms about disrobing and soon we are gathered around our own topless model. This group is mostly European and no one seems to mind a bit of nudity. I soon get over it and focus on my painting.

The pouring rain is tapping on the window and creating a cosy ambience. A supply of tea, coffee, hot chocolate and cake is delivered from the main house. I am busy transferring Michaela's curves onto canvas in a naturalistic and representational style. Xavier, however, is painting in a more abstract manner which takes me a while to interpret.

Being inside means there is no natural time limit so most of us paint until six, then pack up and wander to our respective houses.

Dinner is the usual delicious Caribbean fare, and I find myself looking around the table at the wonderfully chilled out, sun-kissed faces of my art compatriots. Perhaps this business of art and diving vacations is going to work out rather well.

Wednesday and Thursday are reserved for another beach near Bailey Town, and we are given free rein to paint any outside scene or to touch up our live-model paintings. The weather on the first morning is absolutely gorgeous and the group enthusiastically disperses to settle across scenic locations near the shore.

We find a lovely quiet spot at the end of the beach. I am feeling excited about our plans and am dancing exuberantly around Xavier. After ignoring me for a bit, he says he cannot concentrate and unceremoniously hoists me over his shoulder and runs into the sea with me. I am giggling and spluttering while I pull him into the waves and kiss him passionately. We go for a long swim and finally settle down to painting.

Later in the afternoon I find myself staring at the sky-blue ocean. A gentle breeze is whispering through my sarong and the warm sun is softly caressing my face. The teachings of the water-goddess drift into my thoughts. Her natural progression of lessons and my dedicated journaling are finally creating something special.

I close my eyes and listen to the exquisite sound swirling around me. It is dreamy and wonderful … a testimony to discovering and manifesting my inner essence. It is the joyful song of my heart. My Heart Song!

I stroll back to Xavier and plant a kiss firmly on his lips. "I am so happy to be sharing this time with you." There is a growing awareness of the imminent end to this vacation. I resolve to savour every beautiful moment.

* * *

Friday is a day off from the art classes. We stir sleepily on the yacht then slowly awaken with strong coffee and toast. I glance out the window at the brightening sky. Another perfect day in the Bahamas.

We are snuggling together under the duvet when Xavier reaches over to the cabinet and extracts a map. He points to a place in the ocean near the top of North Bimini. "I would like to take you here this morning. I think you will enjoy it."

And so, for the first time, we set sail – southward and around the eastern shore, then northward to a location some distance beyond the island.

He anchors the catamaran and unlocks the cupboard containing scuba and snorkelling gear. I am thankful that the rear of the boat is low against the water, as the fins are ridiculously long. Once they are on my feet I am unable to walk anywhere, only slide gently into the water. After the final checks, we clear our goggles and cruise along the ocean surface.

"We are going to dive now. It's only fifteen or twenty feet to the bottom. The unusual rocks form the Bimini Road and many believe it is one of the outposts of the Lost City of Atlantis. You know, the ancient advanced civilisation."

I look at him quizzically. "No, I don't know." I remember swimming to that submerged crystalline building in the sea near Loutro. Tethys made some interesting comments at the time. I wonder if there is a connection.

Xavier plunges down and I hasten to join him. The 'road' is immediately discernible: a stone formation leading south-west on the ocean floor, running parallel to the side of the island. I hover over the rocks for a few moments, unsure how these indicate an advanced civilisation.

Suddenly a fierce current grips us and sweeps us north past the huge stones. There is nothing we can do but hold onto each other as we are pulled into the yawning sea. The ocean floor is now miles below and I am scared. The current lets us go and I wait for Xavier to signal our next move. We are probably twenty yards under water but it is risky to rise to the surface without careful decompression.

The soft flicker catches my attention. I wave to Xavier and point. A silver figure is swimming toward us with rhythmic movements that create the appearance of a mythical mermaid. It's the water-goddess!

You two are far from home. Have you come for a visit?

I cannot tell if she is being serious or playful. Did she draw us here or is she trying to help us?

Take my hand, both of you. You won't need goggles or mouthpieces.

Now we are diving effortlessly into the deep blue and not breathing. I am as astonished as the first time. Xavier seems more relaxed; perhaps he has done this before. My mind overflows with questions. Is she transferring oxygen to us by some magical osmosis? Why is the increasing water pressure not crushing us?

Far below, the glimmer of a crystalline structure is coming into view. We must be miles deep in the dark ocean. This is insane. I focus on staying calm. Please, please don't let go of my hand …

We float through the shimmering building with Tethys. The massive archway leads into a glowing, translucent courtyard. We are surrounded by magnificent ageless structures embossed with strange hieroglyphic writing. It is a mysterious and awe-inspiring place.

We are right in the middle of what you call the Bermuda Triangle. Much of our great knowledge and technology is hidden here, just waiting for humankind to raise to a higher vibration. At that time, all will be revealed – Atlantis will rise again.

What is she saying? Where did all the pragmatic life-teachings go? I look at Xavier who seems utterly enraptured by the architecture of the building.

We have many submerged cities lying along the Tropic of Cancer longitudinal line. Not just here in the Atlantic Ocean. Have you heard of the Dragon's Triangle running between Tokyo and Taiwan and out into the Philippine Sea? The Atlantean outposts are widely spread.

Wow. Is Xavier listening? I am starting to feel dizzy and overwhelmed. I catch his attention and jiggle my thumb, pointing upwards.

She smiles kindly at me and quickly whooshes us to the surface, returning us to the boat. I clamber aboard and remove the scuba gear. Xavier fetches some still water and a towel. He puts his arm around me while I breathe in the fresh air. The warm sunshine relaxes my body and I soon feel back to normal.

Tethys is hovering alongside the yacht. I can sense a lecture coming.

It's alright, Zara. Earth-beings, water-beings, air-beings, fire-beings … we all have a place. We are simply waiting to meet at the same vibration so we can work together in peace and harmony.

I often wonder if humans realise the huge physiological and psychological stress they have put themselves under by damaging their planet. Do they know how food and water is supposed to taste? How air is designed to invigorate and heal? Instead, environmental stressors have contributed to a worldwide prevalence of poor health, fatigue, anxiety and depression.

Our mother, Gaia, your living earth, is struggling under the strain of air, water and soil pollution, coal and oil extraction, and voracious deforestation. How much longer can she tolerate this violent disrespect? How much longer will she support humankind?

Xavier is listening with keen interest. I reach across to hold his hand.

When you have a moment, place a heading in your journal:
My Global Family

This concept extends far beyond respecting human cultural and ideological differences. Treating all humans with respect, loving-kindness and compassion is only the beginning. You are connected to a global family that comprises all life around you. Plants, insects, animals, the sky, the earth, the elementals –

"The elementals?"

Xavier smiles. "Earth, water, air, fire and aether."

"What's aether?"

"The mysterious fifth substance, the quintessence of the universe."

"Oh."

On your planet, if you discover a corporation or business that is polluting your rivers or airways, tell everyone about it and then stop supporting them. Your cash and cards are influential means to vote your disapproval. Do not purchase goods from companies that harm your planet or that bring suffering.

There is great power in your new social media. It's time for compassionate, caring human beings to connect, talk and share. It's time for empathy and altruism to join with positive action. Spread knowledge virally. Vote with your clicks. Sign online petitions. Demand change.

Make your voices heard. Oppose the cruelty and profiteering of war. Stand against speculative investments designed to siphon money to the wealthy. Campaign for investments that improve worldwide health and education. Campaign for an end to poverty. There are plenty of resources on this planet, more than enough for all. You need to get involved and take responsibility for how your planet's wealth is distributed.

Form groups to discuss how you can positively contribute to society and how you can change and shape your world. Connect with earth-beings who have similar visions and intentions. You are not meant to stand alone. If you wish to change your personal reality, your social reality or your planetary reality, you have to learn to work together. You need to synergise your intentions and collaborate to create a new consensual reality.

She gives a slight bow with her hands in the prayer position. I feel a burst of loving energy and find myself bowing spontaneously in return. Then she is gone, leaving us with much to ponder.

We spend the rest of the day soaking up the sun, discussing the paranormal underwater events and working on our business plans. Should we incorporate the Bimini Road into our scuba and snorkelling vacations? Is it a good idea to weave a spiritual element into our website? I sigh … there is so much to learn and so much we do not know.

The evening is spent making small talk around the dinner table. There is no point mentioning either our business plans or our surreal adventure. It is warm and the wine is flowing. Xavier's fingers are softly caressing my inner thigh, playing a seductive, sweet serenade. I could kiss him madly right now.

The evening feels interminable and when we finally cycle to the yacht, we get no further than the deck before we are wildly kissing in the delicious moonlight. Our caresses are fervent as we tumble into each other's hungry bodies. Soon I am gazing up into his entranced eyes and our hearts are melting into blissful union.

* * *

Saturday is designated as 'group sharing day', a chance to reflect and comment on everyone's artwork. Dave and Michaela will also be giving private feedback to each individual. On top of this, they will choose the best paintings to display in a gallery showing tonight at the Marina Pavilion, a beautiful glass-panelled convention facility at the Bimini Bay Resort. It will be an unframed showing but the resort has excellent wrapping, storage and shipping facilities.

The morning is spent in pleasant conversation. As the assessment approaches, the atmosphere shifts into restless excitement. I have no interest in the judging nor the prize of the pavilion. My mind is on tomorrow, the day the vacation ends. I have no idea when I will see Xavier again. The thought squeezes my heart terribly.

Frustratingly, social and professional requirements sweep the precious day away. In the late afternoon I grab Xavier by the hand and we walk to the nearby beach. There is so much I want to say to him; instead my words splutter through tears: "… afraid … miss you … how will it work … will you wait …"

"Sweetheart, I understand how difficult this is for you. You have some tough challenges ahead. Know that I will support you, whatever decisions you make. I am only an email away."

"Thank you, Xavier. That is so romantic!"

He falls about laughing. "I love you! I wish to share my life with you. You are the other beat of my heart."

"Better," I say in a mock scolding voice.

He takes my hand and looks into my eyes. "I mean it. Hurry back. I can't imagine living my life without you."

"I love you too. You are the man of my dreams." We hold each other for a long time, then sit wordlessly watching the ebb and flow of the sea.

Dave is calling us so we amble over to the gallery. A number of tourists are flocking around, quietly critiquing and admiring the artwork. Waiters swish past, carrying platters of champagne and canapés, while students hover, ready to explain particular aspects of a painting. Xavier manages to sell his abstract nude for a tidy sum and soon one of my paintings is purchased too. The resort deducts a small commission and we decide to put the proceeds into our new business fund.

The event is a great success. Our final group dinner turns into a huge celebration at the Sabor restaurant. We are reposed in an idyllic waterfront setting, admiring the spectacular views, and the champagne is flowing freely amid the delectable courses. There is the faintest hint of sadness interspersed among the jubilant smiles.

It is late by the time we arrive back at the catamaran. I need to sleep here one more night to remind myself that this is my new home. I do not want to make love. I ask Xavier to hold me tight and to hold me all night. We eventually fall asleep, our embrace only broken by the bittersweet light of morning.

I say goodbye to Xavier at his yacht. The tears and smiles say far more than words. We hug each other forever. And then I am crossing an ocean to return to London.

* * *

I last no more than five days, then confess all to Robert. He takes it rather calmly and with great composure, suggesting that I move out of his house before Christmas. "It's too painful for you to be here. I need to be alone."

"I am so sorry," I say, but my words and tears fall onto stony ground. No apology can ease the agony of betrayal and loss.

It is early December. The skies are an incredible grey, filled with icy clouds that appear puffed with outrage. Sadness, fear and guilt are storming inside me. I move my belongings to a friend's garage and pack my suitcase. Farewell is a stoical hug, a monotone "Good luck with your life," and a contrite and useless "I'm sorry. Good luck with yours too."

Lilura has offered her company through the Christmas holidays, a welcome respite from the emotional chaos of my life. After a few days of frosty walks and hot chocolate by the lake, I start to unwind and relax. We cook tasty meals in her warm kitchen, read quietly by the crackling fire, sip whiskey and chat late into the evenings.

We giggle through a gorgeous facial at the local spa, then wander through the clothing shops and gift stores, and eventually patronise a coffee shop renowned for its delicious chocolate cake. When I mention how unsettled I feel about giving up everything, she cleverly reminds me that experiences are far more important than possessions.

A couple of days later I am saying goodbye to Lilura and a worrisome thought pops into my mind. "When will I see you again? I am moving to the other side of the world."

She gives me a tight hug. "Honey, the most important thing is to follow your Heart Song. Everything else will fall into place. I love you very much."

I am driving away and sensing the doors closing behind me. I feel apprehensive but recall the words of the water-goddess: *Remember, faith and doubt will be your steady companions on your path to fulfilment and peace.*

The next three months are strange. I resign from my job – oh so scary – and sell everything I own. Liquidity is important now; I need cash in the bank. I stay in the back room of a friend's house while completing the art classes. Dave is very positive about the new business and dispenses plenty of advice and encouragement. I watch my security slowly dissipating.

I am regularly emailing Xavier to update him about my progress. He knows I cannot move until the advanced class finishes in March. Familiar pings deliver an abundance of loving, supportive messages: 'No, I haven't changed my mind' … 'Yes, I am still waiting for you' … 'I love you with all my heart'. I am probably driving him crazy with my concerns and fears.

By March, I am down to one suitcase of my favourite clothes and a bag containing my laptop and personal documents. It must be the least I have ever owned. I have purchased my ticket to Florida and am ready to step into an uncertain future.

All that's left is the informal graduation ceremony and party. I am sitting in the auditorium waiting for my name to be called out. My mind casts back to the basic art class I commenced three and a half years ago. My, how things have changed. Tethys is right. If you have a clear vision, and patiently and diligently apply yourself –

"Zara?" I walk to the front and collect my diploma. Gosh, that's it. The end of a huge chapter and the beginning of another. The champagne flows and there are celebratory cheers all round. Many of the students have become close friends so I hope we all stay in contact.

At the end of the evening I embrace Dave and walk away from everything I have known. The taxi is waiting outside. I am filled with fluttering emotions. On the way to the airport I close my eyes and take comfort in the sweet serenade of my Heart Song.

* * *

Settling in with Xavier is absolutely wonderful. The yacht is spacious so we manage not to get under each other's feet. It is fabulous living so close to our beloved ocean, sharing meals and cuddling up to each other every night.

The miracle of technology means we can run our businesses from our boat. The new website looks great and enquiries are coming in regularly.

We are adept at balancing our intimate time and our alone time. It's something we both believe is healthy for a relationship. I enjoy cycling to a beach near Bailey Town and sitting quietly by myself, just staring at the waves or writing in my journal. He occasionally works over in South Bimini, which allows him time in his own world.

In June, Xavier gets a request for a yacht delivery. We discuss it at length. The money is very good but he will be away for three weeks. I sigh. Every lifestyle has a price tag. The water-goddess has taught me well. We agree on the work and he flies out with a crew in early August.

I spend this time sketching and painting at Porgy Bay, and even join a small meditation group comprising local Bahamians and foreign residents. After one particularly peaceful session I am chatting to the group leader, Avedis, budding artist and local entrepreneur. He is a lovely man and we share many similar interests.

Avedis mentions that he is struggling with his accommodation business and is looking for someone to invest. He is a Bahamian citizen who owns land with three large houses, one of which is used for the meditation classes. As soon as I show interest, he offers me a tour of the property and the opportunity to appraise the business. The buildings are not as modern and fancy as the resort houses but they are charming and well located with bay-side terraces and mooring.

I recall that you need to purchase property under the International Persons Landholding Act if you wish to apply for permanent residency. And who better to link up with than a Bahamian citizen who has become a good friend? This investment would solve a few personal and business issues in one simple move.

By the time Xavier returns, I am bursting at the seams. I am hugging him, kissing him and bouncing around excitedly. What does he think of this idea? Could it work? Would it be a sensible investment?

We dive off the yacht and go for a long swim together, then return and make beautiful love. He seems unusually quiet today; perhaps he is mulling over the business proposal. At sunset, he reaches into the fridge and extracts a bottle of Moet et Chandon. He takes my hand and leads me to the outside lounging area. Two glasses of sparkling champagne are poured. Then he gets down on one knee, gazes lovingly into my eyes and asks, "Will you marry me?"

I burst into tears. He puts his arms around me. "Hey, sweetheart …"

A joyful smile breaks through my weeping. "Yes, yes. Of course the answer is yes."

It is still for a few moments, then I say, "We can keep it really simple. Your parents are gone, as are mine. Perhaps a wedding on the beach attended by our close friends. And I don't need an engagement ring – it's an antiquated notion. I want us to be equals, each wearing a platinum wedding ring."

"Hmm … I like that very much." He looks at me tenderly and strokes a tear from my face. "I love you."

I grab him, pull him downstairs and we make the most heartfelt love. Then we fall asleep, content in each other's arms.

In the morning I let him sleep. He must be tired from all the sailing and he can be quite moody if he hasn't slept enough. Is this love? Getting to know one's partner and learning when to negotiate and when to accommodate?

I cycle down to Porgy Bay with my sketchpad and journal. Glimmers of light are edging over the horizon. The cool sea invites me for an early swim. I am about fifty yards out when a familiar form swirls before me.

"Tethys!" I move toward her and give her a squelchy hug. "I am so pleased to see you."

It is good to see you too, Zara.

"Look how my life has changed. Xavier and I are getting married. I am living near the ocean. We have started a new business. Thank you so much for all the sage lessons and patient guidance."

I laugh and splash her playfully. "What is it you would like to teach me today?"

There are two exercises to help you complete your transition.

Inscribe this heading in your journal: **Letting Go**

You will need to select one or more people from your past and write them a letter of gratitude. Write this letter in your journal as you will never actually post it. Make sure you answer these questions: What did I learn from our relationship? What were the good experiences? Are there any great memories? Is there anything I wish to say to this person?

When you are finished, I would like you to imagine this person sitting in front of you, and you will read the letter to this person.

"Gosh. Yes, I can do this. I will do it this morning on the beach."

The second exercise is to be completed at the back of your journal. Inscribe this heading: **My Gratitude List**

When you have time, write down ten things for which you are deeply grateful. You also have the option to continue this exercise indefinitely by using every Sunday evening to write down three things from the preceding week for which you are deeply appreciative.

"Is that it? That's sounds easy. I will do it this morning as well. I like the Sunday evening option – it's definitely worth doing."

Peace, Zara.

The water-goddess swishes away, leaving me to swim to shore, dry off and get to work in my journal. The first exercise is incredibly cathartic. I write a letter to Robert and after reading it to him, I feel a tremendous weight shift from my shoulders. The tears are cool and relieving. The letter to my mother and father is very different; there is a melange of anger and sadness but the reading makes me feel closely connected to them.

The morning has melted away. I will do the second exercise on the yacht. I cycle back and get some breakfast going. I can hear he is just stirring.

* * *

We arrange the wedding for early September. It is a simple and beautiful ceremony that fulfils our romantic wishes. A few close friends attend and we celebrate with champagne and canapés on our favourite beach, Porgy Bay.

In October, on my birthday, we sign the deal to partner with Avedis, giving us only eight weeks to refurbish all three properties before the high season, which runs mid-December to mid-April.

It is the first day of December and we have been working flat out. I am adding the last brushstroke to a gorgeous mural in the biggest house, while the guys are applying the final licks of paint to the second-floor outside railing. We pause at lunchtime and agree to take the rest of the day off.

The catamaran is now moored outside our property so Xavier and I climb aboard and set sail. On a whim, I suggest we head out to the Bimini Road where we had our surreal experience with Tethys. He shrugs his shoulders in a 'why-not?' and sets course.

We are just rounding the top of the island when a pod of dolphins begins undulating along each side of the yacht. I look at Xavier, all smiles. It is a glorious sight: the white catamaran on a turquoise sea flanked by these adorable surfers. Our attention is drawn to a silver swirling up ahead and we see the water-goddess beckoning us to follow.

We travel far in a north-easterly direction until the sea becomes an incredible dark blue. The water is eerily calm and flat. The boat is not moving at all. There is only one place we can be. "The Bermuda Triangle," I whisper. Xavier nods solemnly.

Tethys motions to us. *Come with me. Just as you are. The yacht will be here when you return.*

We leap into the water. Him in his white cotton trousers and open-collar shirt and me in a long white cotton dress. She takes hold of our hands and sweeps us down; only her luminescent light keeps us from being enveloped in the increasing darkness.

We arrive at the centre of a shining crystal city. The pillars of a huge building are bathed in a soft, golden glow. Tethys guides us through the archway and lets go our hands.

You will be able to breathe in this building. Go inside, they are waiting for you.

There is a walkway lined with bouquets of white roses, white carnations and white lilies. Bach's Ave Maria is floating sweetly through the air. The red carpet feels velvety beneath our bare feet. I hold Xavier's hand as we walk up the aisle.

A large water-being looms up ahead. He is well built and his full beard flows onto a sumptuous silver robe. The voice is authoritative and powerful.

I am Oceanus, god of the oceans. Do not be afraid. I will not harm you.

I bow instinctively while Xavier asks, "What do you want with us?"

You are here to meet your loved ones and celebrate your union.

There is a deathly still as the music stops. What is he saying? Is he referring to mother?

Zara, I am your father. I had no choice but to leave you. Earth is not my home. Your mother ached for me and chose to join me five years ago. She is alive and well.

I stare at him knowingly. I should be stunned, yet there is a part of me that understands immediately. "Where is mother?"

He moves aside and she appears from behind a silken curtain. "I am here, sweetheart!"

I rush into her arms and we squeeze each other tightly. Tears are streaming down my face. "Mother! Is it really you?"

Oceanus speaks again. *Xavier, your parents are here too. We found them drowning after the boat accident and gave them a choice. They are now water-beings living in our world.*

His parents reveal themselves and he runs to embrace them. They are conversing ardently in a foreign language. I have never seen him cry before and my heart aches when I catch a glimpse of his moist face.

We move to an indoor garden paved with large white stones. It is a dizzying experience and there is much to talk about. "Yes, this is our home" … "No, we cannot return to earth; we are water-beings now" … "Yes, you can visit if Tethys brings you" …

A couple of hours later a water-nymph asks us to return to the main hall where Oceanus is waiting. We hear the compelling voice: *Is everybody ready for the ceremony now?*

A round of nodding heads; then a harp and flute commence Mendelssohn's Wedding March. I look at Xavier. His eyes are still weepy but he is smiling lovingly at me and reaches out to gently clasp my hand.

We are standing in an awesome stateroom, wearing perfectly appropriate outfits, surrounded by our loved ones. Oceanus proceeds with a beautiful marriage ceremony, interspersed with inspirational messages from our families. This is beyond my wildest imaginings and I am deeply grateful.

The next few hours are spent in impassioned conversation until a water-nymph floats across and announces that it will soon be dark on the surface. After tearful farewells and promises to see each other again, Tethys escorts us back to the yacht.

We sail home animatedly discussing the incredible day. By the evening we are both exhausted, managing only to nibble an avocado salad before collapsing into bed. I kiss Xavier goodnight. "This is the best day of my life. I love you." He holds me close as he drifts into sleep. "Mine too …"

* * *

We wake up late Sunday morning in rather reflective moods. Exhilaration and happiness seem counterpointed by sadness and a ream of questions. After a hearty breakfast we cycle to Porgy Bay and sit on the beach. It is another glorious, sunny day and a fresh breeze is gently teasing our relaxed bodies.

We chat for a while then lay outstretched on our backs, making sand angels. He rolls across and passionately kisses me. "I love you, my darling wife ... Come on, let's go for a swim." It's a race to the water and a flurry of arms and legs as we immerse ourselves in the aquamarine sea. We swim about two hundred yards out then float and gaze at the island. I am smiling brightly. I adore living here. I love sharing my life with Xavier.

We are playing in the ocean when a single dolphin joins us. It is lively and high-spirited and we sense an empathic connection immediately. Together we dive underwater then bounce along the waves, whooping joyfully. The beautiful marine creature disappears and moments later pirouettes into an astounding, ultraslow cascade through the air. A magnificent feeling flows through me.

Then we hear the words: *Always remember your* **legacy**. *What have you inherited? What are you giving to the world? What will you leave behind when you are gone?*

We watch as the dolphin moves toward the shore, losing sight of it behind a curling wave. The beach comes into view again and we notice a figure standing in the shallow water. He is wearing a long silver robe and his radiant white hair cascades over his shoulders.

By the time we arrive on the shore, he is away. There are no footprints to be seen anywhere. We walk up the beach and find a huge heart drawn in the sand, surrounded by musical notes.

Inside are inscribed these words:

**Do what you love,
love what you do,
and be with the one
who is right for you.**

I hold Xavier's hand as our mellifluous Heart Songs exquisitely intermingle. The sun is warming our backs as the swoosh of the sea softly swirls around us. A marvellous sensation is coursing through our beings. Is it hope? Is it faith? Is it love? Is it deep peace? Or is it absolute joy?

Stephen Shaw's Books

Visit the website: www.i-am-stephen-shaw.com

I Am contains spiritual and mystical teachings from enlightened masters that point the way to love, peace, bliss, freedom and spiritual awakening.

Heart Song takes you on a mystical adventure into creating your reality and manifesting your dreams, and reveals the secrets to attaining a fulfilled and joyful life.

They Walk Among Us is a love story spanning two realities. Explore the mystery of the angels. Discover the secrets of Love Whispering.

The Other Side explores the most fundamental question in each reality. What happens when the physical body dies? Where do you go? Expand your awareness. Journey deep into the Mystery.

Reflections offers mystical words for guidance, meditation and contemplation. Open the book anywhere and unwrap your daily inspiration.

5D is the Fifth Dimension. Discover ethereal doorways hidden in the fabric of space-time. Seek the advanced mystical teachings.

Star Child offers an exciting glimpse into the future on earth. The return of the gods and the advanced mystical teachings. And the ultimate battle of light versus darkness.

The Tribe expounds the joyful creation of new Earth. What happened after the legendary battle of Machu Picchu? What is Christ consciousness? What is Ecstatic Tantra?

The Fractal Key reveals the secrets of the shamans. This handbook for psychonauts discloses the techniques and practices used in psychedelic healing and transcendent journeys.

CPSIA information can be obtained
at www.ICGtesting.com
Printed in the USA
BVHW072237290120
570848BV00005B/487

9 780956 823724